JOURNAL FOR THE STUDY OF THE OLD TESTAMENT
SUPPLEMENT SERIES
151

JSOT Press
Sheffield

The Citizen–Temple Community

Joel Weinberg

Translated by
Daniel L. Smith-Christopher

Journal for the Study of the Old Testament
Supplement Series 151

Published by JSOT Press
JSOT Press is an imprint of
Sheffield Academic Press Ltd
343 Fulwood Road
Sheffield S10 3BP
England

Typeset by Sheffield Academic Press
and
Printed on acid-free paper in Great Britain
by Biddles Limited
Guildford

British Library Cataloguing in Publication Data

A catalogue record for this book is available
from the British Library

ISBN 1-85075-395-X

CONTENTS

ACKNOWLEDGMENTS

The chapters in this book originally appeared as follows:

Chapter 1
'Bemerkungen zum Problem, "Der Vorhellenismus im Vorden Orient"', *Klio* 58 (1976), pp. 5-20.

Chapter 2
'Demographische Notizen zur Geschichte der nachexilischen Gemeinde in Juda', *Klio* 54 (1972), pp. 45-59.

Chapter 3
'Das *Bēit 'Ā bōt* im 6.–4. Jh. v.u.Z.', *VT* 23 (1973), pp. 400-14.

Chapter 4
'Der *'ammē hā'āreṣ* des 6.–4. Jh. v.u.Z.', *Klio* 56 (1974), pp. 325-35.

Chapter 5
'*N^{e}tînîm* und "Söhne der Sklaven Salomos" im 6.–4. Jh. v.u.Z.', *ZAW* 87 (1975), pp. 355-71.

Chapter 6
'Die Agrarverhältnisse in der Bürger-Tempel-Gemeinde der Achämenidenzeit', *AAASH* 12 (1974), Fasc. 1-4.

Chapter 7
'Zentral- und Partiukulargewalt im achämenidischen Reich', *Klio* 59 (1977), pp. 25-43.

ABBREVIATIONS

AASOR	Annual of the American Schools of Oriental Research
AAASH	*Acta Antiqua Academiae Scientiarum Hungaricae*
AfO	*Archiv für Orientforschung*
AJBA	*Australian Journal of Biblical Archaeology*
AJSL	*American Journal of Semitic Languages and Literatures*
AO	*Der Alte Orient*
ArOr	*Archiv Orientálni*
BA	*Biblical Archaeologist*
BASOR	*Bulletin of the American Schools of Oriental Research*
BBR	In the Days of the First Temple [Hebrew]
BHT	Beiträge zur historischen Theologie
BM	Biblical Motifs, Origins and Transformations
BWANT	Beiträge zur Wissenschaft vom Alten und Neuen Testament
CIS	*Corpus Inscriptionum Semiticarum*
DKHHLH	Publications of the Fifth World Congress of Jewish Studies [Hebrew]
EB	*Encyclopaedia Biblica*
E-I	*Eretz-Israel*
ERR	Y. Aharoni *et al.*, *Excavations at Ramat-Rahel I-II*, Rome, 1962–1964
FRLANT	Forschungen zur Religion und Literatur das Alten und Neuen Testaments
HTR	*Harvard Theological Review*
HUCA	*Hebrew Union College Annual*
IBK	Innsbrucker Beiträge zur Kulturgeschichte
IEJ	*Israel Exploration Journal*
JAOS	*Journal of the American Oriental Society*
JBL	*Journal of Biblical Literature*
JNES	*Journal of Near Eastern Studies*
JSS	*Journal of Semitic Studies*
KSGVI	A. Alt, *Kleine Schriften zur Geschichte des Volkes Israel*
Leš	*Lešonénu*
MBJW	Sh. Yeivin, *Studies in the History of Israel and his Land* [Hebrew]
NAA	*Narody Azii i Afriki*
Numen	*Numen: International Review for the History of Religions*

NKGWG	Nachrichten von der königlichen Gesellschaft der Wissenschaften zu Göttingen
OBO	Orbis biblicus et orientalis
OBS	Oriental and Biblical Studies
OTMS	The Old Testament and Modern Study
PEQ	*Palestine Exploration Quarterly*
PHLHB	Publications of the Israelite Society for Bible Studies [Hebrew]
PJ	*Palästina Jahrbuch*
PS	*Palestinskij Sbornik* [Russian]
RE	*Paulys Real-Encyclopädie der classischen Altertumswissenschaft*
RevQ	*Revue de Qumran*
RSO	Rivista degli Studi Orientali
SBL	Society of Biblical Literature
VDI	*Vestnik drevnjej istorii* [Russian]
VT	*Vetus Testamentum*
VTSup	*Vetus Testamentum*, Supplements
VuH	*Verbannung und Heimkehr*
ZAW	*Zeitschrift für die alttestamentliche Wissenschaft*
ZDPV	*Zeitschrift des deutschen Palästina-Vereins*

TRANSLATOR'S FOREWORD

I first became familiar with Joel Weinberg's work while I was writing my dissertation at Oxford University. I was immediately impressed with his work and began to correspond with him. The decision to translate this collection of essays was taken in the course of the years of correspondence that followed. As his work became the topic of increased interest in the Society of Biblical Literature, the need for this translation grew more serious. Careful readers will note many changes in the English text when compared to the German articles previously published. It must be understood, however, that all the changes were introduced into the drafts by Weinberg himself, or discussed in consultation between us. The International Research Exchanges Board (IREX) generously supported this translation project by making a travel grant available to enable me to go to Latvia in December 1991 and consult with Weinberg on this manuscript. At that time, he presented me with his own English translation of the final chapter that appears in this book, which updates and summarizes his thesis. I was also able to discuss this work, and its history, at some length. The comments that follow are based on those discussions. Unfortunately, I cannot read Russian, so many of these comments will remain informal, due to my inability to confirm many of the points made by direct reference to the authors mentioned. Although this is perhaps less than scholarly, I believe that nevertheless these comments may prove interesting and may encourage the more linguistically prepared to pursue a more detailed investigation of the history of the 'temple community' concept among scholars of the former Soviet territories.

The Intellectual Context of Weinberg's Contributions

From 1933, when the pioneering Soviet Assyriologist V.V. Struve constructed his thesis summarized in 'The Problem of the Genesis,

Development, and Disintegration of the Slave Societies in the Ancient Orient',[1] to the present, the work of (formerly) Soviet historians has increased in interest to students and scholars of ancient history, and more recently, biblical studies as well.[2] Approaching the study of ancient history from suggestions in early Marxist historical theories, the Soviet school was typified by a particular interest in questions such as social relations and social status, authority structures, pre-capitalist forms of economic production and the relationship of empires and their economic systems.

The most influential Soviet ancient historian was clearly I.M. Diakanoff, the founder of Near Eastern studies in St Petersburg. Although not an orthodox Marxist himself, he sought to develop some of the historical theories of the early Marx—most specifically the differences between pre-capitalist 'modes of production'. Included in such pre-capitalist categories were the Greek/Hellenistic polis, and the 'Asian' or 'Oriental' mode of production. Diakanoff tried to be more critical with regard to these terms, and define regional differences more specifically. (These remarks and those that follow are based on comments made by Weinberg, during an interview in December, 1991 in Daugavpils, Latvia.)

Diakanoff accepted the existence of such a pre-capitalist system, but suggested that there were three variations, associated with different geographical and historical areas: (a) Mesopotamia, (b) Egypt and (c) Classical civilization. The differences are to be seen in their respective agrarian relations, that is, the relative size and importance of state versus private lands, as well as the status of the members of society. In Mesopotamia, most citizens were free and fully-enfranchised, and slavery remained a relatively minor sector of society. In Egypt, most workers were in some sense dependent, while in Classical societies there were large numbers of both dependent and independent labourers. What is also important in Diakanoff's work is the differentiation between 'class' and 'estate' in ancient society. There is a difference between the estates of free, partly-free and slave on the one hand, and on the other in whether individuals possessed land and worked it themselves, possessed land with others working on it, or did not

1. Reprinted in English in I.M. Diakanoff (ed.), *Ancient Mesopotamia* (Moscow, 1969).

2. H.W.F. Saggs, *The Greatness that was Babylon* (New York, 1962), p. 508.

possess land and were forced labourers. Thus, we see examples of how Diakanoff attempted to be more precise about questions originally posed by Marx.[1]

Diakanoff's students have taken his interest in differing, and interesting, directions. One example is the work on slavery in Babylonian materials by M. Dandamaev.[2] Often, these students continue the critical tradition established in Diakanoff's work. Pierre Briant, for example, reviewed Dandamaev's recent work thus:

> [Dandamaev] discusses with great lucidity the fundamental problem of whether Babylonia of that time was a slave society. He refers several times to the theoretical controversy surrounding this question in the Soviet Union, and has no hesitation in rejecting some of the positions held there. . .[3]

Another line of development in Soviet historiography can be seen in the concept of 'the temple community'. The development of this concept, and its application to certain ancient Near Eastern societal forms of the first millennium, can be traced to two important influences within Soviet historiography: Marxist notions of pre-capitalist society, and even more interestingly, ethnographic studies of tribal society in pre-Christian Caucasus mountain villages.

To trace the roots of the 'temple community' concept in Caucasian tribal confederations seems a very similar theoretical development to, for example, the amphictyony concept from classical sources in the work of Noth, or the tribal confederation model of N. Gottwald drawn from Iroquois Native American social formations. Weinberg specifically mentioned the work of V.V. Bardavelidze, whose study, 'The Administration of the Hefsurian Community', was published by the Georgian Academy of Sciences in 1952. On the basis of

1. Some of Diakanoff's concerns are seen in the English essay in *Ancient Mesopotamia*, 'The Rise of the Despotic State in Ancient Mesopotamia'.

2. See M. Dandamaev, 'State and Temple in Babylonia in the First Millenium BCE', in E. Lipiński (ed.), *State and Temple Economy in the Ancient Near East* (Orientalia Lovaniensia Analecta, 6; Leiden, 1979); 'Social Stratification in Babylonia (7–4 Century BCE)', in *Wirtschaft und Gesellschaft im Alten Vorderasien* (Budapest, 1976); 'The Neo-Babylonian Elders', in *Societies and Languages of the Ancient Near East* (Festschrift I.M. Diakanoff; 1982).

3. P. Briant, 'Chattel-Owning Chattels' (review of *Slavery in Babylonia from Nabopolassar to Alexander the Great [626–331 BCE]*, by M. Dandamaev, *Times Literary Supplement*, Oct. 17, 1986), p. 1173.

ethnographic observations of pre-Christian villages in the Caucasus Mountains, the 'temple communities' were settlements based on a local temple as its centre which operated the local economy, and was also at the centre of all political and social, as well as religious, life. But the concept was further explored as a way of understanding Hellenistic societies in Mesopotamia by G. Sarkisian in 'The Self-Governing City in Seleucid Babylonia'.[1] Sarkisian was interested in the combination of Hellenistic socio-economic forms with older Mesopotamian forms. One feature of this combination was the unification of a local population with a local temple, such as those found in Uruk, Borsippa and Babylonia. In the Seleucid period, these towns had a form of self-government where the temple was the leading organization. In other work, Sarkisian also explored the revival of clan concepts in Hellenistic/Mesopotamian societies, as well as the ideology of considering 'God' or 'the gods' to be the actual 'owners' of the property of the community (which was, of course, the ideological foundation of administration).[2] Sarkisian's work was developed by two East German scholars: B. Funck in his 1975 Leningrad dissertation,[3] and J. Oelsner in his 1970 Jena dissertation.[4]

Another line in the development of the temple community concept was taken by A. Perichanian. In the 1950s, she worked on epigraphic materials of Asia Minor published by Ramsey. Using also classical sources such as Strabo, Perichanian discussed autonomous local organizations in Asia Minor in the Hellenistic period, in Comana, Zela and Pessinous (Galatia). Perichanian's work on Asia Minor agreed with Sarkisian's work on Mesopotamia in key elements such as the role of the temple, the ideologies of divine ownership of land and the use of land among the community members. Perichanian was also interested in the status of the workers in these autonomous 'temple

1. G.Ch. Sarkisian, 'The Self-Governing City in Seleucid Babylonia' [Russian], *VDI* 1 (1952).

2. In a letter to the translator in June 1992 Sarkisian denies it was the Caucasian/Armenian anthropological material that influenced his formulation, as Weinberg suggests, but late Babylonian texts themselves.

3. B. Funck, *Uruk zur Seleukidenzeit: Schriften zur Geschichte und Kultur des Alten Orients: Eine Untersuchung zu den spätbabylonischen Pfundentexten als Quelle für die Erforschung der sozialökonomischen Entwicklung der hellenistichen Stadt* (Berlin: Akademie Verlag, 1984).

4. J. Oelsner, 'Studien zur babylonischen Kultur und Gesellschaft in hellenistischer Zeit' (Jena University, 1986).

communities', but her most important contribution is the thesis that the temple community concept had its roots in pre-Hellenistic, and possibly even pre-Persian, social formations. The key is in identifying the increasing or decreasing role of the temple in these communities.

In 1955, J.D. Amusin first applied the 'temple community' concept to the postexilic Judaean community in his article, 'The People of the Land',[1] but he did not develop this thesis. Here is where Weinberg's own work fits into the evolution of the concept, because his own dissertation (largely reproduced and translated in the work that follows) picked up and developed Amusin's suggestions.

Weinberg's use of the 'temple community' concept seeks to define a socio-economic unit which involves religious affiliation to a temple and priesthood, and secular authority by royal patronage of the temple, thus binding people together in a temple 'economy'. Weinberg seeks to further develop the sociological implications of this entity, and, in doing so, is one of the few scholars dealing with the exile event who takes seriously the disrupting nature of this military defeat and deportation.[2] A similar idea was independently developed by H.D. Mantel, in his study, 'The Dichotomy of Judaism during the Second Temple',[3] and in my opinion, Mantel's work deserves more recognition in the development of scholarly work on the nature of the postexilic community.

Whether one agrees or not with the specific lines of the 'temple community' concept when applied to the postexilic Judaean community, Weinberg argues convincingly that the postexilic community underwent significant social and ideological changes, and the basic social formation, the *bêt 'ābôt* (house of the fathers), is in fact an entirely new social structure in the Persian period that is helpfully outlined by the 'temple community' concept. The questions surrounding the forms of postexilic Judaean society are clearly relevant to a modern understanding of the Bible, since most modern critics date the final composition (and an increasing number the very writing) of the Bible in the postexilic era, and therefore a product of this postexilic Judaean community. Finally, on a personal note, there are clear differences between the ethnographic and socio-psychological models

1. J.D. Amusin, 'The People of the Land', *VDI* 2 (1953).

2. I develop this in my work, *The Religion of the Landless* (New York, 1989).

3. H.D. Mantel, 'The Dichotomy of Judaism during the Second Temple', *HUCA* 44 (1973).

of deported peoples that I continue to work with in my own analysis of the exile, and Weinberg's 'temple community' model, but they are certainly not entirely incompatible.

It is impossible to discuss Weinberg's work without taking note of the current events which have changed world circumstances faster than most of us can totally comprehend. It is important to mention, therefore, the tortuous path of biblical studies in the former Soviet territories. Until the death of Stalin, it was forbidden to work on Jewish history, and this continued to be a subject under great suspicion afterwards. The work here largely translated into English was originally destroyed in the Soviet Union. Weinberg's work was denounced by a colleague as 'Zionist propaganda' and the Russian manuscripts and printer's galleys actually destroyed. Weinberg could thereafter only publish in Soviet republics such as Georgia and Armenia which had no official policies of anti-Semitism. In the 1960s, he was able to publish two books on Old Testament themes in Latvia, in the Latvian language.

East Germany presented further complications. Although there was some official anti-Semitism, the pressures of West Germany's public 'philo-Semitism' created an atmosphere where some important work in biblical Jewish history could be published—most notably the work of H. Kreissig. In East Germany, for example, an edition of Josephus was published, but a recent translation into Russian was never published.

For Weinberg, the darkest years were under Brezhnev. Latvian authorities nonetheless allowed articles to be mailed abroad, if one had arranged to have special permission to show the post office when mailing manuscripts. The late Professor P.A.H. de Boer was instrumental in seeing Dr Weinberg's first article published in the West, 'Das *Bēit 'Āḇōt* im 6.–4. Jh. v.u.Z.', in *VT* (1973).

Now, of course, the situation is dramatically changed for scholars like Weinberg. His new work on Chronicles (in German) is presently being negotiated for publication in the West. The work represents an attempt to see this historical composition as an expression of the world-view of the Judaean 'citizen–temple community' and thus will be an important further development of the concepts first elaborated in the present volume. Another work now in Russian will probably become available in English, *The Birth of History: The Idea of History in the Near East in the Middle of the First Millennium.* Future projects, according to Weinberg, include an *Einleitung*, which will investigate the various world-views of the different literary genres of the Old Testament.

It has been a great pleasure to be part of this effort to further dialogue in biblical studies, and I wish to thank Dr Philip Davies and the Sheffield Academic Press for their interest and patience. I remain responsible, of course, for remaining errors, and apologize for occasional difficulties in the English readings, some of which stem from the different writing styles in Eastern European scholarly discourse, especially under the influence of Marxist categories and concepts.

I wish to dedicate this translation to Joel and Lujba Weinberg. Weinberg's life of heroic scholarship humbles those of us in the West whose trials pale in comparison, and I know he would agree that it would not have been possible without Lujba Weinberg's support. We can only be thankful that circumstances now make dialogue between Eastern European and Western (especially American) scholars so much easier.

Editor's Note: No attempt to supplement the bibliography in these essays has been made, nor have the references to Weinberg's original publications been amended when they have been translated in this volume. Readers are asked to appreciate the practical difficulties involved and to accept the limitations imposed on the translator and editors by the physical circumstances of this volume's execution.

Daniel L.S. Christopher
Los Angeles, CA

Chapter 1

COMMENTS ON THE PROBLEM OF 'PRE-HELLENISM IN THE NEAR EAST'

When Droysen introduced the concept of 'Hellenism' into historical-scientific literature over one hundred years ago, he could hardly have been aware that this would become one of the 'perennial questions' in the study of the ancient world. Generations of historians have worked toward a clarification of this phenomenon and it is one which concerns modern historiography as well, because clarification of the nature of Hellenism is essential for the understanding of the ancient world.

Modern Marxist views of the study of Hellenism can be classified in the following way:

'Hellenism is a step in the history of ancient slave-economies... a historically necessary result of the previous evolution of ancient Greece', wrote Ranovitch[1] at the end of the 40s. This assessment of Hellenism rose, through Konrad,[2] to a universal interpretation. According to his view, the Hellenic monarchies of the Eastern Mediterranean, the Roman republic as *hegemon* of the Western Mediterranean and the reign of the Tsin Dynasty, were typologically comparable phenomena which were called into being by the crisis of the city-state at the end of the second phase of slavery formation in the ninth to eighth to the third to second centuries BCE. The tendencies within these phenomena worked toward the formation of socio-political units other than the city-state and presaged the arrival of the third phase of slavery formation.

Against this conception of Hellenism as a step in ancient slave

1. A.B. Ranovitch, *Hellenism and its Historical Meaning* [Russian] (Moscow, 1950), p. 16.

2. N.I. Konrad, 'On the Slave-Holding System', in *Collected Works on History* [Russian] (Moscow, 1974), pp. 203-205.

economy, or as a universal world-historical epoch, Zeljin already commented in 1953, 'Hellenism is not an epoch of the whole civilized world of ancient history... Italy and the lands west of the Mediterranean cannot be seen as part of the Hellenistic world—nor India or China.'[1] In another place Zeljin defined Hellenism 'as a process of unification and mutual impact in different cultural areas of the local traditions (primarily affecting local socio-economic relations) and Greek and Macedonian foundations'.[2]

Kreissig represents another standpoint which derives from the conception that there are basically only two pre-capitalist modes of production. The 'ancient' mode's main features are unlimited private ownership by fully-enfranchised citizens of the means of production, and the total alienation of producers (slaves or dependent workers) of the means of production, and their full mobilization. The second is the 'Asian' serf/bondage-based mode of production, where the producers are in the possession of the means of production, while the rights of higher ownership of these means of production belong to a privileged group or class, who, using non-economic power, force the workers to produce a surplus product. While the Hellenic polis employed the 'ancient' mode of production, the Hellenistic states outside Greece represented the 'Oriental' mode of production. Although Kreissig admits to a certain limited interaction between both modes of production in both areas during the Hellenistic epoch, he emphasizes that 'such forms remain exceptions. There is no general economic convergence.' Recognizing the expansion of the polis in the Hellenistic area, he denies the existence of the Hellenistic polis in general, stating that there was only a Hellenic polis in the realm of old classical Greece (that is to say, in its classic formation), while in the realm of the ancient Oriental states the polis had its own form.[3]

Although these three conceptions of Hellenism diverge significantly, they have in common the view that Hellenism was a system which

1. K.K. Zeljin, 'The Main Features of Hellenism' [Russian], *VDI* 4 (1953), pp. 145-47.

2. K.K. Zeljin, *Studies on the Agrarian Relations in the Hellenistic Egypt in the 2-1 Centuries*, BCE [Russian] (Moscow, 1960), p. 435.

3. H. Kreissig, '"Antike" Produktionsformen im hellenistischen Asien, "Orientalische" Produktionsformen in der klassischen Ägäis', *Acta Conventus XI* (Warsaw, 1971), pp. 42, 45; 'Die Polis in Griechenland und im Orient in der hellenistischen Epoche', *Hellenische Poleis*, II (Berlin, 1974), p. 1082.

entailed economic, social, political and cultural factors. In other words, Hellenism required historically necessary and objective pre-conditions, and a pre-Hellenism came before Hellenism.

An understanding of pre-Hellenism obviously relates to the corresponding conception of Hellenism. For Ranovitch[1] it is obvious that 'the causes of the origin and establishment of Hellenism are to be sought in the essential contradictions within the slave-based society of ancient Greece', while for Kreissig[2] the main point is the internal evolution of the 'bondage-based' mode of production, but any scholar who agrees with Zeljin's conception of Hellenism must speak about a 'pre-Hellenism' in Greece and Macedonia, and a 'pre-Hellenism' in the Near East.

The multifaceted aspects of the evolution of Greece and Macedonia in the fourth century BCE were recently investigated very thoroughly.[3] Therefore this study is concerned only with pre-Hellenism in the Near East, and the attempt is made to discuss some phenomena in the Near East which preceded Hellenism in this area and set the stage for in the middle of the first millennium BCE.

In the scholarly literature, it is still debated whether Alexander harboured a plan of world domination or not, and if so, the time of the inauguration and failure of such a plan.

Much more important is the related problem of the sources and roots of such a plan of conquest of the world and world domination. The historical reality of Greece could not have contributed concrete examples to the Macedonian ruler and his surroundings, but in the Near East there were political formations which could have served as a model for such a plan—namely the world empires of the first millennium BCE.

In the historical evolution of the Near East, the first millennium BCE occupies a special place, because it significantly differs from the previous millennium, particularly in the structure of the economy, the society, the state and culture.[4] One of the notable characteristics of the

1. Ranovitch, *Hellenism*, p. 17.

2. H. Kreissig, *Die sozialen Zusammenhänge des judäischen Krieges* (Berlin, 1970), p. 26; *Die sozialökonomische Situation in Juda zur Achämenidenzeit* (Berlin, 1973), pp. 20-34.

3. L.M. Gluskina, 'On the Specificity of the Greek Classical Polis in Connection with its Crisis' [Russian], *VDI* 2 (1973), pp. 27-42.

4. I. M. Diakanoff, 'The Main Economic Features of the Monarchies of Ancient

first millennium BCE is the presence of so-called 'world empires'—the neo-Assyrian, neo-Babylonian and Achaemenid—whose developments were defined by the necessity of a compulsory exchange of raw materials which was the result of the uneven development of the different regions in the Near East, and also the result of a backward economy.[1]

These world empires, especially the Achaemenid, could offer a model to the Hellenism of the future, a model containing some of the solutions to problems unknown to the classical polis, such as the construction of central and local power and the relationships between them. The central power in the Achaemenid empire was constituted from the central bureaucratic administrative apparatus, with the king at the top, under whom were royal offices, many different functionaries and a widely dispersed 'state police'. Local institutions also belonged to the the central administration—the satrapies with the satraps, their offices, scribes and officers, and also the provinces with the *peḥâ* at the helm. Local administration consisted of the self-administered, autonomous areas within the satrapies and provinces. The frames of autonomy and the forms of the self-administration were multifaceted, defined as they were through peculiar historical developments of the affected regions, and through the dominant local traditions. A numerous and notable group of self-administered organizations were the Greek polis of Asia Minor, which maintained not only its familiar institutions under Persian rulership, but also the groupings of cities in a religio-cultic league (Herod. 1.147-49). The situation was similar with the cities of Phoenicia, the rulers of Caria, Paphlagonia, and elsewhere, while most of the tribes—the Arabs (Herod. 3.88) or the Colchians (Herod. 3.97) for example—knew only a nominal Persian control. The most notable type of autonomous structure was the citizen–temple community of the sixth to fourth centuries, whose relation to the central power (and vice versa) was to anticipate the coming Hellenistic states in many ways.

Although the Achaemenid empire, like its predecessors, was capable of organizing forced economic exchanges and population movements, the Achaemenids—especially after 518—put an end to unbridled

Western Asia' [Russian], *NAA* (1966), pp. 44-58; Diakanoff, 'The Main Features of Ancient Society', *The Problems of Pre-Capitalist Societies in Eastern Countries* [Russian] (Moscow, 1971), pp. 142-43.

1. N.B. Jankovskaya, 'Some Economic Problems of the Assyrian Empire' [Russian], *VDI* 1 (1956), pp. 28-46; Diakanoff, 'Main Features', pp. 133-34.

exploitation and the plundering of the dependent peoples. The new system of state taxes that Darius I initiated obliged all satraps to pay the required taxes—determined for each area by a consideration of the size of the cultivable land and the quality of its fruitfulness. The taxes were paid in silver and thus the new system stimulated the development of a money economy. Since only a limited number of satrapies possessed silver mines (e.g. Sardis, Cilicia), the remaining satrapies had to sell their agricultural or manufactured goods, in order to secure silver to pay the taxes. So, the residents of Yehud brought taxes-in-kind, *leḥem happeḥâ* (Neh. 5.14), which was possibly gathered in the form of a tithe.[1] A part of the tax-in-kind was used for maintenance of the court of the satrap, the administration and the soldiers of the governor, while the other part was stored in the royal storehouse and was exchanged by the governor or treasury officials for silver and sent as taxes to the state treasury.[2]

The neo-Assyrian and neo-Babylonian rulers practised compulsory mass deportations of the conquered populations, whereas the Achaemenid used such measures only in extremes, and relatively seldom as punishment (e.g. Herod. 6.3). The majority of these deported peoples enlarged the number of the workers in the royal estates where, for example, in 509–494 BCE (in 108 places in Persia and Elam) about 21,575 *kurtaš* of different ethnic composition served, including Egyptians, Babylonians, Indians, Greeks and Thracians.[3] Free individual or collective migration, however, was more important than the forced deportations for demographic, socio-economic and cultural processes in the Achaemenid Empire. Many traders, craftsmen and 'intellectuals' settled in the rising centres of the Empire. Thus, Persians, Medes and Aryans lived in Nippur; Arameans, Elamites, Lydians, Greeks, Phrygians, Carians, Arabs and Egyptians in Babylon; and in Susa, Elamites, Persians, Babylonians, Jews, Greeks and others. In some cities (Babylon, Nippur, Memphis)

1. M.A. Dandamaev, 'Politische und wirtschaftliche Geschichte: Beiträge zur Achämenidengeschichte', ed. G. Walser, *Hesperia* (Einzelschriften) 18 (1972), pp. 43-45.

2. M.A. Dandamaev, 'The Temple-Tithe in Late Babylonia' [Russian], *VDI* 2 (1965), pp. 14-34.

3. M.A. Dandamaev, 'Workers in the Royal Estates in Iran from the End of the Sixth to the First Half of the Fourth Centuries BCE' [Russian], *VDI* 3 (1973), pp. 3-26.

these foreigners lived in specific parts of the city where they had their own assembly and administrative organization. In most cases, however, the foreigners lived side by side with the native population, marrying among them, switching many times from one religion to another, or worshipping native and foreign gods simultaneously.[1] Thus, an 'inner Near East' ethnic mix prevailed in the atmosphere of intensive migration processes of the sixth to fourth centuries BCE. This involved mainly the people of the Near East. Greeks of the Aegean did not take an active part, although the Greek colonization of the southern coast of the Black Sea still continued. The Near Eastern element that dominated the migration process also decisively influenced the emergent levelling of evolutionary progress as well as a growing rapprochement of the different types of economy and society in the Near East. This was decisive for the emergence of 'pre-Hellenism' in these places.

Before the Near East was enveloped in the Persian empire, societies existed at different stages of socio-economical and political development. Some examples are the Arabs or the tribes of the north-eastern and central area of Asia Minor and the population of the Armenian highlands. In Iran, Syria, Western Asia Minor and other places, societies without large scale irrigation were dominant, with an agricultural economy and a predominantly communal private sector of the economy. In southern Mesopotamia a society flourished on the basis of largescale irrigation with a developed commodity economy and dominant state economic sector, while on the coast of Asia Minor one found Greek cities with highly developed money economies based on slave-labour.

The incorporation of these various societies in the Achaemenid empire, the duration of a relative peace within its boundaries, the system of taxation and the intensive road building, the active migration process, and still other factors, called forth a marked rate of increase in production and a growing rapprochement of the level of economic development in the Near East.

Essential changes are noteworthy in the main branch of production, which was agriculture, but they were especially remarkable in the area of handicrafts. It is superfluous to refer to the well-known increase of manufacturing in the old centres of Mesopotamia, Egypt

1. Dandamaev, 'Politische Geschichte', pp. 56-58.

and Phoenicia. More important for 'pre-Hellenism' in the Near East is the development of manufacturing in the lands which were stagnant previous to this time, for example Judah and Colcia. The increase in productivity in these areas depended on the positive influence of the progressive centres. For example, for Judah it was mainly the eastern centres[1] which were a major stimulation to economic development.

The rise of agriculture and manufacturing, and also the Achaemenid taxation system, were closely bound to the flourishing trade of the sixth to fourth centuries BCE that involved those areas of the Near East which previously (as in Judah) were shut out or hardly touched. In the sixth to fourth centuries BCE, Judah imported precious metal and wood, precious stone and ceramic, textiles and spice, aromatics, for example, and exported balsam, asphalt, wheat, oil and other things. A centre of this active trade was Jerusalem,[2] but the numerous finds of Greek ceramics and Southern Arabian products in Engedi, Lachish, and other places proves not only that these peripheral cities participated in trade, but also demonstrates the wide-reaching trade relations of Judah with Arabia, Egypt, Phoenicia, the Aegean and Asia Minor. In the trade of the previous millennium, particularly foreign trade, the royal sector was predominant. But in the sixth to fourth centuries BCE, private traders dominated, as is shown by the activity of the trade houses of *Egibi* and *Murašu* where trade was associated with banking and land ownership.[3]

The ancient era began with the birth, and ended with the death, of the old city,[4] but there were times of intensive urbanization which alternated epochs of decline. The Achaemenid period was an epoch of active urbanization, but evidence for this is to be found not only in the old centres of citied life—Mesopotamia,[5] Phoenicia, or in Western Asia Minor—although even there, a growth of the city was also

1. E. Stern, 'The Land of Israel in the Persian Period' [Hebrew], *Qadmoniot* 2 (1969), pp. 114-24.

2. J.P. Weinberg, 'The City in the Palestinian Citizen–Temple Community of the 6–4 Centuries BCE' [Russian], *City and Trade (III to I Millennium BC)* (Yerevan, 1973), pp. 152-53.

3. M.A. Dandamaev, 'The Role of the Tamkar in Babylonia of the 2–1 Millennium BCE' [Russian], *City and Trade*, pp. 65-77.

4. I. M. Diakanoff, 'The Problems of the Babylonian City in the 2 Millennium BCE' [Russian], *City and Trade*, pp. 30-34.

5. R. McAdams and H.J. Nissen, *The Uruk Countryside: The Natural Setting of Urban Societies* (Chicago, 1972), p. 56.

remarkable in the sixth to fourth centuries BCE. Much more meaningful is the urbanization process in the areas where the majority of the cities were previously destroyed, for example in Judah, or where early cities were generally not present, for example in Colchis or Iberia. In Judah, where the Babylonians had destroyed almost all of the southern cities, there were only nineteen cities (already before 458–457) in the area of the citizen–temple community, a number which grows to more than forty cities at a later time.[1]

The cities of the Palestinian citizen–temple community, as also others in the Achaemenid Near East, had an internal self government, which was led by the *ziqnê ʿîr* (elders of the city), *šōpᵉṭîm* (judges), and assembly of the citizens, and so on. These organs of self-administration took over judicial functions, organized the defence of their city, and the like. Although this organization of the urban self-administration reveals a certain similarity to the classical Greek polis, the Near Eastern city is not typologically comparable to the polis.[2]

In the system of Near Eastern pre-Hellenism, a meaningful role developed for the characteristic socio-political organism which is indicated by the term 'temple community', or, more precisely, 'citizen–temple community'. This organism, which came into being early in the first millennium BCE, grew particularly intensively in the Achaemenid period. The citizen–temple community existed in Asia Minor (e.g. Komana, Olbia, Pessinus, Zela) and Armenia (e.g. Tordan, Ani) Mesopotamia (e.g. Uruk, Borsippa, Nippur), Syria (e.g. Bambyke, Emessa), Phoenicia and Palestine.

The appearance and the expansion of this form of community was influenced by the socio-economic development of the Near East, particularly by the evolution of the royal and private/communal sectors of the Near Eastern economy. In the sixth to fourth centuries BCE, one notices perceptible and significant changes in agricultural relations.[3] On the first level is the expansion of the property of the Achaemenid lands, although the assumption that the king was considered the theoretical owner of the entire land is false. Hundreds of slaves (*kurtaš* or *garda*) worked on the Achaemenid estates which were

1. J.P. Weinberg, 'Demographische Notizen zur Geschichte der nachexilischen Gemeinde in Juda', *Klio* 54 (1972), pp. 54-57.
2. Weinberg, 'The City', pp. 153-56.
3. Diakanoff, 'Main Economic Features', pp. 132-33.

located on royal properties.[1] A part of the royal lands were leased to dependent farmers (*ikkaratu*), but soldiers were also settled on them. Those who managed the portions assigned to them had to fulfil military requirements and to pay certain taxes either in money or in kind.[2]

From the estates of the conquered kings and the unruly aristocrats, the Achaemenids gave portions as a gift to members of the royal family, members of the Persian nobility, high officials and other so-called 'benefactors' of the king. These persons were given a hereditary possession which was also free from royal taxation. These great land possessions (for example, the numerous estates of Arsames in lower and upper Egypt, as also in six different areas between Susa and Egypt, the properties of Tissaphernes in Phrygia, and others) were worked by slaves. Among these slaves were some that had families, and possessed houses and moveable goods—and in juridical life they were handled as fully enfranchised citizens.[3] The royal estates, the properties of the elite, settlements of the dependent farmers, and fiefs of the soldiers, together composed the royal sector of the economy as opposed to the private–communal economy. The latter encompassed the tribal lands, the numerous village settlements and the extensive temple properties.

The growth of production and the development of the commodity–money economy, the strengthening of trade and the active urbanization led to the point where, by the sixth to fourth centuries BCE, both sectors developed similarly individualized economies.

Thanks to this similar economic organization, there was a unification of the representatives of both sectors (mainly in the cities) and a reduction of the social differences between them. This process also promoted the physical and geographical unification of both sectors. In Nippur, for example, the royal estates and properties of the Persian nobility, temple estates and estates of the trade-houses such as *Murašu*, were all close together.[4] However, the decisive circumstance was that

1. Dandamaev, 'Politische Geschichte', pp. 27-33; *Slavery in Babylonia in the 7th–4th Centuries BCE* [Russian] (Moscow, 1974), pp. 44-390.

2. M.A. Dandamaev, 'Temple-Farmers in Late Babylonia' [Russian], *PS* 17 (1967), pp. 41-49; *Slavery*, pp. 341-44.

3. M.A. Dandamaev, 'Testimonies of Slaves in the Court in Babylonia in the 6th Century BCE' [Russian], *VDI* 1 (1968), pp. 3-12.

4. Dandamaev, 'Politische Geschichte', pp. 30-31.

already in the second half of the second millennium many temples (for example in Barsippa) were autonomous and privileged organizations, which possessed self-government, and were almost, or even fully, independent of the central administration. The neo-Babylonian rulers collected no taxes from them; instead they were given funds.[1]

In these temples, conditions permitted many possibilities for the development of private activities in land deals, manufacturing and trade. In the sixth to fourth centuries BCE the tendency for the development of private activities and initiative was encouraged by the growth of production and encompassed not only the elite of the so-called 'royal people', but all those who could deal with an expansion of their activities, mainly in a commodity economy. There were many who were interested in separating from the royal sector, particularly in the conquered areas where this sector dominated and dependence on them was marked.

Under these circumstances of the sixth to fourth centuries BCE, the separation from the royal sector was best carried out by a unification with the temple. Through this unification of a city community and a temple, an essentially new structure was built—the citizen–temple community, which was a unified organization of community members and the priesthood of the temple. This citizen–temple community gave its members an organizational unity and collective self-government, and provided for internal political, social and economic welfare.[2]

In the sources of the Achaemenid period the postexilic community of Palestine is the best documented citizen–temple community. This community will serve as a model for the reconstruction of this socio-political organization, although comparable information will be drawn from other Near Eastern citizen–temple communities. Since different aspects of the Palestinian community have been discussed in other studies, only a summary of the most characteristic aspects of the citizen–temple community will be given here.

Demographic data are decisive for determining the importance and meaning of the citizen–temple community in the Near Eastern parts of the Achaemenid empire. For the Palestinian community, the data can be seen as follows:[3]

1. M.A. Dandamaev, 'The Temple and the State in Late Babylonia' [Russian], *VDI* 4 (1966), p. 35.
2. Diakanoff, 'Main Economic Features', p. 133.
3. Weinberg, 'Notizen', pp. 53-57.

	Before 458/457	Percentage of Total Population	*After 458/457*	Percentage of Total Population
Community members	42,360	c. 20	15,000	c. 70
Cities	19		c. 50	
Isolated areas	3		6	

Although for the other citizen–temple communities in the sixth to fourth centuries BCE such precise figures are not available, there is sufficient proof that many of these structures, for example the temple–community of Zeus Chrysaoros (Caria), the community in Pessinus (Phrygia), in Comana, Zela and others (Pontos) and in Olba (Ciliciōa),[1] had extensive territories and not insignificant numbers of residents. We can thus conclude that the citizen–temple community was, purely quantitatively, an element of Near Eastern pre-Hellenism that should not be underestimated.

The members of the Palestinian citizen–temple community, no less than those in Asia Minor, Armenia, Mesopotamia and other places,[2] were divided into two groups—laity and priesthood. The available information permits a relatively precise social picture of the Palestinian community in the middle of the fifth century BCE.[3]

	Designation of Group	Collectives	Men	Percentages
1	'Men of the people of Israel'	17 (32)*	16722/15520†	54.9/53.2
2	Collectives named after localities	14/16	8684/8635†	28.5/29.6
3	Priests	4+3 (20/21)	4289	14.2/14.7
4	Levites	1 (8)**	74	0.2
5	Singers	1	148/128†	0.5/0.4
6	Gatekeepers	6 (6)	138/139†	0.4/0.5
7	*n^e^tînîm* 'sons of slaves of Solomon'	42/45	392	1.3/1.4

* The numbers in brackets apply to after 458/457.

** We only know the general numbers for levites and singers.

† The first number is from Nehemiah 7, the second from Ezra 2.

The non-priestly part of the membership of this community is

1. Weinberg, 'Notizen', pp. 57-58.
2. Weinberg, 'Notizen', p. 52.
3. J.P. Weinberg, 'Das *Bēit 'Āḇōt* im 6.–4. Jh. v.u.Z.', *VT* 23 (1973), pp. 404-12.

composed of 'men of the people of Israel',[1] the 'collectives named after localities',[2] and also (as I will argue below) the *n^{e}tînîm* and 'sons of slaves of Solomon', all of whom compose 84% of the community members in the middle of the fifth century BCE.

The 'priests', 'levites', 'singers' and 'gatekeepers' belong to the priestly section, all of whom compose about 16%. Before 458/457, according to their number in the community, the priests played only a secondary role. Afterwards the situation essentially changed, when the number of collectives of priests grew by three times, the Levites by four times. The ratio between the laity and priesthood changed from 5.4:1 before 458/457 to 1:1.2 after 458/457. In the established Palestinian citizen–temple community, as also in the other Near Eastern communities, the priesthood was a dominant and leading power. But it should be stated that often people belonged to the priesthood who had no religio-cultic function, and that 'priest' was frequently a conventional, and not always a professional, designation.

In the Palestinian citizen–temple community the *bêt 'ābôt* composed the basic structural unit by which (before 458/457) the 'men of Israel' and the 'priests' were divided, but after 458/457 the *bêt 'ābôt* embraced all social and professional groups of the community.[3] There is a typological similarity between the *bêt 'ābôt* and the agnatic group in other citizen–temple communities (for example, the *syngenia* in Asia Minor or the clans in Uruk).[4] Therefore it can be concluded that the agnatic group composed the basic structural element of all citizen–temple communities, which was closely bound up with the specifics of agricultural relationships.

The land of the Palestinian citizen–temple community was formally considered to be the property of Yahweh (e.g. Neh. 9.8, 36), but in the sixth to fourth century BCE the Jerusalem temple possessed no land or economy.[5] The land of the community was de facto unalienable property, that is, *'aḥuzzâ naḥ^{a}lâ,* of the *bêt 'ābôt*. The land was divided

1. Weinberg, *'Bēit 'Āḇōt'*, pp. 400-14.
2. Weinberg, *'Bēit 'Āḇōt'*, p. 414.
3. Weinberg, *'Bēit 'Āḇōt'*, p. 414.
4. A.G. Perichanian, *The Temple Communities of Asia Minor and Armenia* [Russian] (Moscow, 1959), pp. 173-74; G. Ch. Sarkisian, 'Self-Governing City in Seleucid Babylonia' [Russian], *VDI* 1 (1952), pp. 79-80.
5. J.P. Weinberg, 'Die Agrarverhältnisse in der Bürger-Tempel-Gemeinde der Achämenidenzeit', *AAASH* (1974), pp. 481-84.

into parcels which were in use by families within the *bêt 'ābôt* and were individually managed by these families.[1]

The studies of Dandamaev, Sarkisian and Perichanian[2] prove that, in all Near Eastern citizen–temple communities of the sixth to fourth century BCE, the corresponding god was considered the overall owner of all the land, but this indication was a convention. In reality the land of the community, or the majority of it, was in use by all the community members. Beside these basic similarities for all citizen–temple communities, some meaningful differences can also be pointed out. Agrarian relations in the citizen–temple communities diverged mainly in two ways: existence or non-existence of temple-land, and existence or non-existence of a temple economy.

On the basis of these criteria, all citizen–temple communities can be divided into three typological groups:

Group A-1 includes the communities whose temple was *de facto* the owner of land and whose land, was divided among the members of the community, but partly self-managed—for example, the communities in Uruk, Sippara, Comana, Zela, Akilisene.

Group A-2 contains the communities whose temples were *de facto* owners of lands, but did not run their own economy. All temple lands were in use by the community members, for example, the community in Mylasa-Olymos.

Group B is composed of those citizen–temple communities whose temples owned no land nor maintained their own economy, for example, the Palestinian community.

Although these three groups exemplify variations in an essentially similar type of agrarian relationship, the differences affected the composition of the temple income, the structure of the temple staff.

The members of the Palestinian citizen–temple community and the other communities of this type composed a society of free and fully-enfranchised people who were socially and politically relatively similar, and who strictly distanced themselves from all those who were not community members[3]. But the *tôšāb* (guest) and *śākîr* (day-workers), who were probably free people, also lived on the land of the

1. Weinberg, 'Agrarverhältnisse', pp. 484-85.

2. Dandamaev, 'Temple', pp. 82-104; Sarkisian, 'Self-Governing City', pp. 68-83.

3. J.P. Weinberg, 'Der *'am hā'āreṣ* des 6.–4. Jh. v.u.Z.', *Klio* 56 (1974), pp. 325-35.

Palestinian citizen–temple community, although they did not belong to the community and had no rights to land. However, they worked on the estates of the community members where slaves were also exploited (some 18% of the community members).[1] In the other citizen–temple communities, particularly of group A, the number of temple slaves was much greater, including the *širkutu* in Mesopotamia[2] and the *hierodouloi* in Asia Minor,[3] as also the number of dependent farmers—the *ikkaratu* in Mesopotamia and the *hieroi* in Asia Minor.

The emergence of the citizen–temple community as the regional power in the Achaemenid Empire was only possible because of the nature of this kind of socio-political organism, but was also influenced or modified by other factors—such as the internal development of each individual community in its own respective territory, and the politics of the central power. The benevolent attitude of the Achaemenid central power to the locally organized citizen–temple community was generally conducive to local development (keeping in mind the occasional and local variations), because the Achaemenids were correct in surmising that this form would be more loyal in comparison with the other formations such as the polis, dynasty or tribe. Such a benevolent attitude, together with the internal development of the corresponding citizen–temple community, led to the unification (perhaps in the form of a personal union) of the local and central power in the person of the resident high priest, who stood at its head (which is logical, given the nature of this formation with the temple at the centre).

According to Sarkisian,[4] the citizen–temple community was 'a type of slave-holding collective, whose other variety is represented by the Hellenistic polis', while Perichanian[5] defended the view that the temple community of Asia Minor and Armenia was 'a more interesting and peculiar type of community which combined elements of eastern and ancient communities', which acquired ever more Hellenistic forms in further evolution and thus could eventually not be differentiated

1. J. Weinberg, 'Slaves and Other Categories of Dependent Men in the Palestinian Citizen-Temple Community of the 6th–4th Centuries BCE' [Russian], *PS* 25 (88) (1974), pp. 63-66.

2. Dandamaev, 'Temple-Farmers', pp. 41-49; *Slavery*, pp. 273-324, 341-65.

3. Perichanian, *The Temple Communities*, p. 117.

4. Sarkisian, *Tigranakert* [Russian] (Moscow, 1960), p. 6.

5. Perichanian, *The Temple Communities*, p. 177.

from the Hellenistic polis. But the agrarian relations, the agnatic group as the main structure and other specific features of the citizen–temple community, differentiate this form from the structure of the classical polis. Although these differences contradict an uncritical typological comparison of the classical polis and the Near Eastern citizen–temple community, it must be acknowledged that in the citizen–temple community of the sixth to fourth centuries BCE there were structural elements whose similarity with the polis cannot be denied; for example, the exclusivity of the membership, the organization of the local administration, and so forth. These similarities were also contributory to the formation of Hellenism.

There appear then, new developments in the cultural life of the Achaemenid Near East. Four factors played a particularly decisive role. They were the inclusion of the entire Near East in the Achaemenid Empire, the active migration process, the intense ethnic interaction and an active synthesis in all spheres of life.

In the previous millennium, the Near Eastern intelligentsia was constituted exclusively from priests and scribes who were directly related to the state and/or temple. In the sixth to fourth centuries BCE, a significant number of priests and scribes belonged to the structure of the citizen–temple community. At the same time, the number of scribes from lay circles increased, circles which were far from the corporate spirit of the priesthood. These latter circles were not as conservative as the priests and turned greater attention to human individuality and the individual's responsibilities.

These scribes were the agents of the promotion of the Aramaic language to the *lingua franca* of the Empire—an important development for the cultural life of the Near East.[1] In most areas—for example in Syria and Mesopotamia, Aramaic was a colloquial language of the population, concurrent with, and most of the time superseding, the local languages. This officially sanctioned expansion of Aramaic was an important promoter of syncretistic tendencies, but it also created active, zealous opposition—for example in the Palestinian community—where there was a struggle for the purity of the old Hebrew language. This result is similar to the temple communities of Mesopotamia, where the Akkadian language was cultivated. On the linguistic plane, the intermingling of the universalistic and particularistic

1. E. Lipiński, *Studies in Aramaic Inscriptions and Onomastics* (Leuven, 1975), p. 12.

tendencies stood out, and this penetrated the whole cultural life of the Achaemenid Near East—but was especially characteristic for the evolution of Near Eastern religions.

The implementation by the Achaemenids of a religious policy of toleration, in any case in the lands outside of Iran,[1] furthered a remarkable syncretism in the sixth to fourth centuries BCE, which boosted a tendency toward monotheism among the polytheistic religions. In Yahwistic monotheism or in Zoroastrian dualism, this also furthered trends toward universalism.[2] This universalistic tendency co-existed in the citizen–temple communities with a particularism[3] which emphasized the connection of the collective with its god, the recognition of the chosenness of the community, and so on. This particularism was a necessary accompaniment of a community which ideologically justified its autonomy and exclusivity.

Such a co-existence and interaction of both universalism and particularism influenced the Near Eastern literature of the sixth to fourth centuries BCE, especially the creations of the postexilic Palestinian community. Although in many places in the postexilic sections of the Old Testament one finds familiar Old Testament themes (the all-powerful God with unlimited rule over all humanity, or only the chosen community; and the dependence of all humanity, or only the chosen, on God), a new motif was also heard, mainly in so-called Wisdom literature. The teaching of Wisdom literature[4] deals with righteous and virtuous living, and calls upon people as individuals. Wisdom discusses the meaning of humanity and its works, without denying godly will and providence. With this, however, the important Old Testament tension between 'God's will' and 'human freedom' was intensified—a tension which also played such an important role in Hellenistic ideology.

In the eastern Mediterranean there were two epochs of particularly

1. M.A. Dandamaev, *Iran during the Reign of the First Achaemenids* [Russian] (Moscow, 1963), pp. 245-46.

2. W. Röllig, 'Die Religion Altsyriens', *Theologie und Religionswissenschaft* (Darmstadt, 1973), pp. 94-100; M. Weinfeld, 'The Universalistic Tendency and the Particularistic Tendency in the Times of Return' [Hebrew], *Tarbiz* 33 (1964), pp. 228-42.

3. W. Baumgartner, 'The Wisdom Literature', *OTMS*, pp. 210-37.

4. W.A. Irwin, 'The Hebrews', *The Intellectual Adventure of Ancient Man* (Chicago, 1946), pp. 274-75; J.D. Amusin, *The Dead Sea Scrolls* (Moscow, 1960), pp. 175-76.

active and productive contact between Greece and the Near Eastern lands—the second millennium BCE and the time of Hellenism.[1] It was not an accident that many creators of Hellenic culture—Thales, Anaximandros, Anaximenes, Heraclitus, Hecataeus, Herodotus, among others—come from Asia Minor where active contacts with the culture, education, and wisdom of the Near East accelerated the evolution of Hellenic culture. In the seventh to fifth centuries BCE the impact of Near Eastern culture on Greek culture was fuller and more intensive than that of Greek culture on the culture of the Near East, although elements of Greek art are certainly to be seen in Asia Minor seals and in sculptures in Susa, Persepolis and elsewhere.[2]

In sum, then, 'pre-Hellenism in the Near East' is a 200-year historical development of this area when the following preconditions for Hellenism took shape: (1) a remarkable increase of production and a relative equalization of the links of socio-economic development, (2) an expansion of the commodity–money economy, (3) active urbanization, (4) a political unification in the realms of centralizing empires, (5) expansion of the self governing local powers, one of which was the citizen–temple community, (6) intensive inner Near Eastern migration and (7) interaction of—and opposition to—universalism and particularism, and (8) a cultivation of human individuality.

Near Eastern 'pre-Hellenism' was as crucial for the establishment of Hellenism as the economic, social, political and cultural development of Greece and Macedonia in the fourth century BCE.

1. P.A. Grincer, 'Two Periods of Literary Relations' [Russian], *Typology and Literary Interrelations in the Ancient World* (Moscow, 1971), p. 10.

2. N.M. Nikulina, 'On "Eastern-Greek" and "Greek-Persian" Art' [Russian], *VDI* 3 (1969), pp. 106-20.

Chapter 2

DEMOGRAPHIC NOTES ON THE HISTORY OF THE POSTEXILIC COMMUNITY IN JUDAH

It has been quietly assumed in modern biblical studies that the terms 'Judah' and the 'postexilic community' correspond; that is, that Judah in the period of the Achaemenids (sixth to fourth centuries BCE) is considered to be the territorial boundary of the postexilic community. But just because a notion is generally assumed does not mean that it has been scientifically proven.

The attempt to determine more precisely the nature of the citizen–temple community requires a more careful examination of the problems which have already been discussed in biblical studies from Hölscher to the more recent work of Kreissig;[1] that is, the demographic problems of Judah in the Achaemenid period. The significance of these problems warrants further investigation mainly because a detailed answer to these questions is of basic importance to the study of further issues, for example, property relations in the community, the city in the community system, and the struggle between the community and the *'am hā 'āreṣ*.

The natural starting point for the investigation of such demographic questions is the sparse data about the population of the state of Judah. From 2 Kgs 15.19-20 and other sources, the population of the Northern Kingdom of Israel in the second half of the eighth century was approximately 500,000–700,000.[2] Meyer, Lurje, Rudolph,

1. G. Hölscher, *Palästina in der persischen und hellenistischen Zeit* (Berlin, 1903), pp. 3-50; H. Kreissig, *Die wirtschaftliche Situation Judas zur Achämenidenzeit* (Berlin, 1969), pp. 37-43, 60-66.

2. M. Lurje, *Studien zur Geschichte der wirtschaftlichen und sozialen Verhältnisse im israelitisch-jüdischen Reiche*, I (Giessen, 1927), pp. 111-12; R. de Vaux, *Les institutions de l'Ancien Testament* (Paris, 1958), p. 104.

Janssen and other scholars[1] assumed that the population of Judah was much less, since the southern kingdom was smaller and less densely populated. Furthermore, archaeological data confirm the population of Judah to be approximately 220,000–250,000 residents between the eighth and sixth centuries BCE.

In the first half of the first millennium BCE in Palestine, large cities such as Lachish, Gezer, and others, had an area of some 7.2 ha and nearly 6500–7000 residents. Most of the cities were of middle size (2.5–4.0 ha and 2000–4000 residents) and small villages also existed (about 0.4–1.0 ha and 400–1000 residents).[2]

In the town-lists in Josh. 15.21-62 and 18.21-28, which reflect the administrative and territorial divisions of the Judaean state,[3] 150 dwelling places are enumerated, which resulted in a population of approximately 220,000–250,000.

In order to determine the number of those deported from Judah in the years 597, 586 and 582 BCE, it is useful to bring together the contradictory evidence cited by the Old Testament:

Deportation		2 Kings		Jeremiah		2 Chronicles	
		Source	Total	Source	Total	Source	Total
I	597	24.14	10000	24.1	-	36.6	-
		24.16	8000	52.28	3023		
II	586	25.11	-	39.9-10		36.20	-
				52.29	832		
III	?	25.26	-	43.5-6	-	-	-
IV	582	-	-	52.30	745	-	-

Total Exiles:	2 Kings	18,000
	Jeremiah	4600
	2 Chronicles	8000–10,000

Table 1

These contradictory figures have brought about a wide-ranging discussion in modern scholarship. According to Meyer,[4] almost the

1. E. Meyer, *Die Entstehung des Judentums* (Halle, 1896), pp. 108-10; Lurje, *Studien*, pp. 111-12; W. Rudolph, 'Sanherib in Palästina', *PJB* 25 (1929), p. 67 n. 27; E. Janssen, *Juda in der Exilszeit* (FRLANT, 51/69; Göttingen, 1956), p. 28 n. 1.

2. O. Tufnell, *Lachish III (Tell ed-Duweir): The Iron Age* (London, 1953), p. 34.

3. A. Alt, 'Judas Gaue unter Josia', *KSGVI*, II, pp. 276-88; Y. Aharoni, 'The Province-List of Judah', *VT* 9 (1959), pp. 225-46.

4. Meyer, *Entstehung*, pp. 110-14.

whole population was deported from Judah—which does not correspond to the data regarding the situation in Babylonian Judah. Nikel, Sellin and Klausner[1] added the evidence of 2 Kings and Jeremiah and multiplied the result by the number of family members (average five) and concluded that the number of exiles was 50,000–70,000, which would be approximately a third of the residents of Judah. This calculation, however, also contradicts the facts of the situation in Babylonian Judah. If one takes the view of Albright and Janssen[2] that only Jeremiah 52 is believable, and the total number of exiles is 4600, then it becomes difficult to account for the significant number of those who returned from exile after some 60 years. There is much to be said for Mowinckel's[3] assumption that only the number of those from Judah outside Jerusalem is given in Jeremiah 52, while nearly 8000–10,000 people from the capital were led away—resulting in a total of between 12,000 and 14,000 exiles.

The assumption of Mowinckel, which Kreissig[4] agreed with, can be confirmed on wider grounds as well. In 2 Kings mainly exiles from Jerusalem are enumerated (24.14-15; 25.11, 19), whereas in Jeremiah, Judah is predominantly mentioned as the place from where people were deported (52.27, 30).[5] In the first half of the first millenium BCE the area of Jerusalem spread over barely 4.6 ha.[6] which corresponds to a population of 4000–4500. But in a time of war, the population of the fortified capital would increase, so that the phrase, 'and all of Jerusalem was led away' (2 Kgs 24.14), involved 10,000 exiles from Jerusalem, which confirms the view of Mowinckel.

1. J. Nikel, *Die Wiederherstellung des jüdischen Gemeinwesens nach dem babylonischen Exil* (Freiburg, 1900), pp. 3-7; E. Sellin, *Studien zur Entstehungsgeschichte der jüdischen Gemeinde nach dem babylonischen Exil* 2 (Leipzig, 1901), pp. 104-107; J. Klausner, *The History of the Second Temple I* [Hebrew] (Jerusalem, 1954), pp. 33-34.

2. W.F. Albright, 'A Brief History of Judah from the Days of Josiah to Alexander the Great', *BA* 9 (1946), pp. 1, 4-5; Janssen, *Judah*, pp. 28-36.

3. S. Mowinckel, *Studien zu dem Buche Ezra–Nehemia* 1 (Oslo, 1964), pp. 93-98.

4. Kreissig, *Wirtschaftliche Situation*, pp. 38-42.

5. Compare the opinion of A. Malamat, 'A New Record of Nebuchadnezzar's Palestinian Campaigns', *IEJ* 6 (1956), pp. 246-56—that in Jer. 52.28 and 2 Kgs 24.12 two different deportations in the year 597 are mentioned and that the first one involved only inhabitants of the Judaean periphery.

6. Tufnell, *Lachish*, p. 34.

So, it would be safe to say that the total number of the exiles, plus the emigrants,[1] was about 20,000, or some 10% of the population of Judah.[2] Therefore the conquest of Judah did not massively reduce the population. One must also keep in mind that the Judaean population was partly augmented by the Ammonites and Edomites, among others penetrating into Judah.[3] But the repeated deportations would be decisive for the changes that were brought about in the social structure of Judaean society, which are demonstrated by the data in the following table:

Deportation	Identity of the exiles	Source
I 597	Royal court	2 Kgs 24.12, 15
	Judaean aristocracy	2 Kgs 24.14; Jer. 24.41
	Soldiers and officers	2 Kgs 24.14, 16
	Artisans from Jerusalem	2 Kgs 24.14, 16; Jer. 24.1
II 586	Representatives of the priestly and non-priestly elite	2 Kgs 25.18-20; Jer. 52.10
	'The rest of the people left in the city' (Jerusalem)	2 Kgs 25.11; Jer. 39.9; 52.25
	60 men from the *'am hā'āreṣ*	Jer. 52.25

Table 2

Such a resulting profile corresponded to the goal of the Babylonian conquerors not only to exterminate or weaken the elite of the conquered land, but also to maintain the productive potential of land and people.[4] But the groups of deported were also conditioned by pre-exilic socio-political structures.

Recent archaeological work proves that at the beginning of the sixth century BCE, the southern part of the state of Judah was almost totally destroyed, while in the northern part, that is, in the area of the tribe

1. B.-Z. Lurje, *The Jews in Syria at the Time of the Return, the Mishnah and the Talmud* [Hebrew] (Jerusalem, 1957), pp. 7-12.

2. An indirect argument is afforded by the conclusion of E. Stern ('The Land of Israel in the Persian Period' [Hebrew], *Qadmoniot* 2 [1969], p. 114) that 70–80% of all the ceramics found in Babylonian Judah belonged to the local, pre-exilic type.

3. B.-Z. Lurje, 'Edom according to the Prophets at the Time of the Return', *PHLHB* 2 (1956), pp. 95-98; Kreissig, *Wirtschaftliche Situation*, pp. 57-59.

4. I. Mendelsohn, *Slavery in the Ancient Near East* (New York, 1949), pp. 92-95.

of Benjamin, evidence of such a devastation is not obvious.[1] Many towns of Northern Judah—Gibeon, Bethel, Mizpah, for example—remained undisturbed or were only partially destroyed and temporarily abandoned. Such a basic discrimination between two areas of the same enemy state by a conqueror is no accident, but is determined by the different attitudes of the population or various groups in the Judaean and Benjaminite lands toward the Babylonians.

'Private' stamps on pottery, which reveal ownership by the Judaean nobility,[2] are seldom found in the lands of the Benjaminite tribe. The fact that the majority of these stamps come from the area of the tribe of Judah strongly suggests that in the seventh to sixth centuries the aristocracy was mainly composed of representatives of the upper strata in the land of Judah. The influential clan of the Achborites also belonged to this Judaean nobility, whose members held important offices in court and in the army.[3] The Achborites represented an outspoken pro-Egyptian political perspective, as is shown in the direct participation of the Achborite Elnathan, son of Achbor (Jer. 26.20-23); or Yikbaryahu, son of Elnathan (I Lach. 3.15-18; 6.5-7) in the murder of the pro-Babylonian prophet Uriah, son of Shemyahu.[4]

This outspoken pro-Egyptian orientation of the Judaean Achborites is not a chance appearance. The recent archaeological finds from southern Judah prove that this part of the Judaean state was tightly united with Egypt economically[5] and this also influenced the political sympathies of the majority of the Judaean nobility as well as a part of the *'am hā'āreṣ*. The *'am hā'āreṣ* consisted,[6] in the first half of the first millenium BCE, of free, fully-enfranchised citizens who possessed land, served in the militia, and so on. The economic situation of southern Judah, as also a certain unity between the Judaean nobility and the Judaean *'am hā'āreṣ,* strengthened the predominantly anti-Babylonian bias in southern Judah. This expressed itself in the

1. W.F. Albright, *Archaeology of Palestine* (Harmondsworth, 1960), pp. 141-42; G.E. Wright, *Biblical Archaeology* (Philadelphia, 1957), pp. 175-76.

2. M.L. Heltzer, 'Old Palestinian Ceramical Epigraphy as an Important Historical Source' [Russian], *Epigraphica Vostoka* 17 (Moscow, 1966), p. 27.

3. Sh. Yeivin, 'Clans and Parties in the State of Judah' [Hebrew], *MBJW*, pp. 265-67, 279-80.

4. H. Torczyner, G.L. Harding, A. Lewis and J.L. Starkey, *Lachish I (Tell ed-Duweir), The Lachish Letters* (London, 1938), pp. 62-73, 118-19.

5. B. Mazar, 'The Negev in Ancient Times', *IEJ* 4 (1954), pp. 1, 48.

6. J. Amusin, *People of the Land* [Russian], *VDI* (1955), pp. 24-25.

obstinate resistance of the southern cities (e.g. Lachish, Azeqah; Jer. 34.7, I Lach. 4.10-13) to the Babylonian conquerors, and for this reason 'Judah was led away from its land' (Jer. 52.27).

Important communication lines criss-crossed the Benjaminite land[1] where great vineyards produced wine for sale.[2] After the downfall of the Assyrian empire, the old relation between the Benjaminites and Ephraimites was renewed,[3] and the latter areas were already by the end of the sixth century a part of the neo-Babylonian empire.[4] If one keeps in mind that some Benjaminite cities were connected with the local priests who were affected by the reform of 622 BCE,[5] the overriding pro-Babylonian sympathies of the northern part of Judah are understandable. Therefore, a prominent spokesman for the pro-Babylonian bias was the prophet Jeremiah, who came from a priestly clan that was settled since the tenth century BCE in the Benjaminite city Anathoth.[6] Jeremiah's enthusiastic defenders were members of the Shaphanides who were influential at court at the turn of the century.[7] The available Old Testament and epigraphic data shows a relationship between the city Mizpah and the Shaphanides, a member of which was Gedaliah, son of Achiqam, who possibly chose Mizpah as his residence in Babylonian Judah (2 Kgs 25.22-25; Jer. 40.6).

One can conclude that the structure of the exile community depended not only on the aims of conquerors but also on the inner struggles of the Judaean state, the political orientation of different social groups and the territorial divisions of its various factions. The royal court, the residents of the capital Jerusalem, the majority of the Judaean nobility and some of the Judaean *'am hā'āreṣ* were among the

1. Sh. Yeivin, 'Benjamin' [Hebrew], *EB*, II, pp. 275-81.

2. J. Pritchard, 'Industry and Trade at Biblical Gibeon', *BA* 23 (1960), pp. 23-29.

3. J.H. Grönbeck, 'Benjamin und Juda: Erwägungen zu 1. Kön. 12, 21-24', *VT* 15 (1965), pp. 431-36.

4. B. Oded, 'When was Judah Subjugated to Babylon?' [Hebrew], *Tarbiz* 35 (1965), pp. 103-104

5. M. Weinfeld, 'Cult Centralisation in Israel in the Light of a Neo-Babylonian Analogy', *JNES* 23 (1964), p. 206.

6. J. Klausner, 'Why isn't Jeremiah Mentioned in the Book of Kings?' [Hebrew], *MHWA*, pp. 21-46; B. Ufenheimer, 'The Conflict of Jeremiah with the False Prophets' [Hebrew], *PHLHB* 7 (1959), pp. 96-111.

7. They hold the important position *'ᵃšer 'al habbāyit* (H.J. Katzenstein, 'The Royal Steward', *IEJ* 10 [1960], pp. 149-54).

deported. The landless of the south (*dallat hā'āreṣ, hā'ām hadallîm*, 2 Kgs 25.12; Jer. 39.10; 52.16), as almost the entire population of the northern part of the Judaean state, were not affected by the deportation, and this fact decisively influenced the organization of the conquered land by the Babylonians.

In the year 586 BCE the rest of the inhabitants of Judah received some inner autonomy,[1] which was cancelled after the murder of Gedaliah (2 Kgs 25.25; Jer. 41.2-3) in the year 582, when the land of Judah was incorporated in the existing Babylonian provinces in Palestine—mainly Samaria.[2] This caused decades of long struggle between the returnees and the Samarians, and between the returnees and those residents of Judah who were not deported.

The Aramaic version of the edict of Cyrus which initiated the return of the exiles is recognized by many scholars as genuine (Ezra 6.3-5)[3]—while other scholars[4] deny the credibility of the Hebrew variant (Ezra 1.2-4). The Aramaic variant is a *dikrônâ* (Ezra 6.2), a royal order[5] to the Persian office under whom the allocation of money, wool and provisions is administered.[6] Therefore the *dikrônâ* only deals with financial questions—the order to build the temple at the cost of the state and to return the stolen temple wares. In Ezra 1.1, as an introduction to the Hebrew variant, it is said that 'he [Cyrus] caused it to be proclaimed through the entire empire', which means that it was an oral proclamation addressed to the exiles. Therefore, the proclamation was drawn up, and it contained points of concern to the exiles, including the permission to return, the permission to rebuild the temple and the permission to organize a collection in favour of the returning exiles. The Hebrew text is certainly as authentic[7] as the Aramaic, and both are variants on an original that were drawn

1. Klausner, *History*, I, pp. 50-52.

2. A. Alt, 'Die Rolle Samarias bei der Entstehung des Judentums', *KSGVI*, II, pp. 316-37.

3. W.F. Albright, *Recent Discoveries in Bible* (New York, 1956), p. 104; K. Galling, *Studien zur Geschichte Israels im persischen Zeitalter* (Tübingen, 1964), pp. 78-88.

4. M. Noth, *Geschichte Israels* (Göttingen, 1956), pp. 276-79.

5. Ch.F. Jean and J. Hoftijzer, *Dictionnaire des inscriptions sémitiques de l'ouest* (Leiden, 1965), p. 78.

6. M.A. Dandamaev, 'Bagasaru ganzubara', *IBK* 14 (1968), pp. 235-39.

7. E. Bickerman, 'The Edict of Cyrus in Ezra 1', *JBL* 65 (1946), pp. 248-75; J. Liver, 'The Beginning of the Return' [Hebrew], *E-I* 5 (1958) pp. 114-15.

up to correspond to the two different constituencies.

The return of the exiles,[1] permitted by the edict of Cyrus, was not a single event, but rather a multiple and long-lasting process. Additional returns are mentioned in the sources; under the leadership of Sheshbazzar (Ezra 1.11), Zerubbabel (Neh. 7.7 = Ezra 2.2), Ezra (Ezra 8), Nehemiah (*Ant.* 11.5.7) and others. This conclusion is important for understanding that very profitable source of information—the list in Neh. 7.7-69 = Ezra 2.2-67. Modern biblical studies is recognizing the authenticity of this list. This means that only two controversial issues remain, namely the content and purpose of the list.

Some scholars view this list as an indication of the participants in one repatriation in the year 539/538,[2] while others think that it includes repatriations between 539/538 and 515,[3] or all the repatriations from 539/538 until the arrival of Ezra.[4] Still other scholars consider the list to be a census of the population of Judah at the time of Cyrus,[5] or of Nehemiah,[6] while others consider the list as an indication of the members of the community around 519–517[7] or about 400 BCE.[8] According to Albright,[9] the original list contained only an indication of the first returnees, to which later tribes were added as they were accepted into the community from among the local, non-deported population of Judah. If this is the case, then the list as it now appears is a register of the community members from the time of Nehemiah. In my view, the list (whose origin and original form is to

1. The supposition of Torrey (C.C. Torrey, *Ezra Studies* [Chicago, 1910], pp. 285-88; Torrey, *The Chronicler's History of Israel* [New Haven, 1954], pp. xxv-xxviii), that the repatriation is a device of the Chronicler, is flatly denied by modern scholars.

2. Meyer, *Entstehung*, pp. 135-36; H.H. Schaeder, *Esra der Schreiber* (BHT, 5; Tübingen, 1930), pp. 15-23.

3. J. Liver, *The History of the House of David, from the Destruction of the State of Judah to the Destruction of the Second Temple* [Hebrew] (Jerusalem, 1959), p. 87.

4. L.W. Batten, *A Critical and Exegetical Commentary on the Books of Ezra and Nehemiah* (ICC, 26; Edinburgh, 1913), p. 38.

5. J. Wellhausen, 'Die Rückkehr der Juden aus dem babylonischen Exil', *NKGWG* (Klasse, 1895), pp. 176-78.

6. R.H. Pfeiffer, *Introduction to the Old Testament* (NY, 1941), pp. 820-22.

7. Galling, *Studien*, pp. 88ff.

8. Mowinckel, *Studien*, I, pp. 92-109.

9. Albright, *History*, pp. 12-13.

be sought in Neh. 7.7-69) is an indication of the collectives belonging to the 'citizen–temple community' until the year 458/457 BCE.

In Nehemiah 7 = Ezra 2 we find the following evidence of the structure of the community up to 458/457 (Table 3):

Group	Number	Collective	Males % *
1. 'Men of the people of Israel'	17	16,722/15,520	54.9/53.2
2. Collectives named after localities	14/16	8684/8635	28.5/29.6
3. Priests	4	4289	14.2/14.7
4. Levites	1	74	0.2
5. Singers	1	148/128	0.5/0.4
6. Gatekeepers	6	138/139	0.4/0.5
7. *n^{e}tînîm* and 'sons of the slaves of Solomon'	42/46	392	1.3/1.4

* The first number is from Nehemiah 7, the second from Ezra 2.

Table 3

Although there are no clear grounds given for the doubts expressed about the information in the list, one contradiction must be clarified. In the list, only the number of males in the different collectives are given.[1] By adding the individual entries, we have a grand total of 31,089 (Neh. 7) or 29,818 (Ezra 2) men. This contradicts the evidence of Neh. 7.66 = Ezra 2.64—'the whole community to a man was 42,360'.

Klein[2] sought to overcome this contradiction by assuming that the given figures were only the members of the tribe of Judah and Benjamin, while the total also contained the members who belonged to the tribes of Ephraim and Manasseh (cf. 1 Chron. 9.3). Nikel and Klausner[3] attribute the contradiction to the fragmentary nature of the list, while Allrik[4] thought that the original list used an old numerical system that the later editors subsequently misunderstood. On more certain ground, however, are the scholars who suggest that the

1. G.E. Mendenhall, 'The Census List of Numbers 1 and 26', *JBL* 76 (1958), pp. 52-66.

2. Sh. Klein, *The Land of Judah from the Time of the Return from Babylon to the Completion of the Talmud* [Hebrew] (Jerusalem, 1939), p. 2.

3. Nikel, *Wiederherstellung*, pp. 78-80; Klausner, *History*, I, pp. 148-49.

4. H.L. Allrik, 'The Lists of Zerubbabel (Neh. 7 and Ezra 2) and the Hebrew Numeral Notation', *BASOR* 136 (1954), pp. 21-27.

missing 12,000 were women and children[1]—they point out that the concept of *qāhāl* frequently indicated (e.g. Ezra 10.1) the entire community inclusive of men, women and children. But the ratio of 3:1 for men to women/children is abnormal and therefore the hypothesis of Ben-Shem[2] is not without merit, namely that among the returnees young unmarried men were in the majority; and in my opinion this includes the younger members of the exiled families, which is confirmed by the large number of mixed marriages in the community (Ezra 9–10; Neh. 13).

Before 458/457 BCE the emergent citizen–temple community numbered some 42,360 members, that is about 20% of the population of Achaemenid Judah.

In the authentic list of Neh. 11.4-22, men (laity, priests, Levites and gatekeepers) are listed who lived in Jerusalem after the *synoikismos* carried out by Nehemiah. The addition of the individuals named in this list gives a total of 3044 men, corresponding to 15,000 inhabitants of Jerusalem. As the enactment of the *synoikismos* involved the enforced settlement of every tenth member of the community, there is a total of nearly 150,000 community members. This involves an almost fourfold growth when compared with the number of members of the community in 458/457. The growth of community membership after 458/457 was the result of the growing prosperity and security of the community, and of the arrival of new returnees from Babylon, more than from the settled population of Judah. But if it is also assumed that the population of Judah in the course of the century did not decline—and a reduction is hardly conceivable in the light of the reference to the economic growth of Palestine in the fifth century[3]—then the members of the community appeared in the second half of the fifth century to be no more than some 70% of the inhabitants of Judah.

Already these conclusions raise doubts about the equation of the citizen–temple community and Judah of the Achaemenid era. These doubts are strengthened by the following overview of the course of the community's settlement before and after 458/457.

In Palestine, as generally in the Middle East, the city was not only

1. Galling, *Studien*, p. 100.

2. Y. Ben-Shem, 'Sociological Observations on the Return', *PHLBH* 7 (1959), p. 211.

3. Stern, *Land of Israel*, pp. 114ff.

the residence of skilled labourers and merchants, but also of peasants.[1] Around each city was its agricultural region, its *śādôt, migrāšîm* and *ḥ^a^ṣērîm*. The archaeological study of the surroundings of Shechem by Campbell[2] proved that approximately 40 settlements were found around the city within a radius of some 5–6 km, and these were probably buildings for agricultural purposes. The *ḥ^a^ṣērîm* of the south surrounded a city or fortress to which they belonged in an area of approximately 3.5–10 km.[3] Surrounding the Palestinian city of the first millenium BCE, there was 5–6 km of intensive agricultural land, and up to 10 km of land with less intensive agriculture.

In the communication about the repatriation led by Zerubbabel, it is said that 'these sons of the (*m^e^dînâ*)[4]...came out of the Exile...and returned (*wayyāšûbû*) to Jerusalem and Judah, each to his city' (Neh. 7.6 = Ezra 2.1), while Neh. 7.73 = Ezra 2.70 emphasized that the community members lived 'in their cities' (cf. 1 Esdr. 5.45). It is generally assumed[5] that before 458/457 BCE the settlement of the community was restricted to Jerusalem and its nearest surroundings. But against this is not only the plural use of 'the cities', but also the 'collectives named after localities' (Table 3, group 2) whose members (28.5/29.6% of all community members) are listed as residents or part of the residents of 18 cities.[6] But this settlement area is not a closed, unified territory, but rather a situation composed of three isolated regions. The first region consisted of three cities (Lod, Hadid, Ono) in the northern coastal plains. The second region included fifteen cities (e.g. Gibeah, Anathoth, Michmas) located around Jerusalem, and the third region included the Jordan valley with the city of Jericho.

Finally, it should be clarified that inside as well as outside these regions, there were residents who were not a part of this community.

Essential changes in the course of settlement correspond to a

1. I.M. Diakanoff, 'Problems of the Babylonian City in the Second Millenium BCE' [Russian]) (Yerevan, 1973), pp. 34-39; Kreissig, *Situation*, p. 103.

2. E.F. Campbell, Jr, 'The Shechem Area Survey', *BASOR* 190 (1968), pp. 9-41.

3. R. Gophna, '*ḥ^a^ṣērîm* in the Northern Negev' [Hebrew], *Yediot* XXVII (1963), pp. 173-80.

4. In the text *m^e^dînâ* designates the citizen–temple community.

5. Meyer, *Entstehung*, pp. 117-18; Nikel, *Wiederherstellung*, pp. 53-62; Albright, *History*, pp. 7-10.

6. J.P. Weinberg, 'Collectives Named after Localities in Achaemenid Judah' [Russian], *ArOr* 42.4 (1974), pp. 341-53.

significant increase in the community of the fifth century. The lists of Nehemiah 3 and 11.25-36 report these changes. The questions surrounding the veracity of the second list, however, are still open. According to Meyer, von Rad, and others,[1] it is a copy of the town-list in Joshua 15 and 18. For Kellerman, on the other hand, this list is an indication of the last strong contingents of the Judaean kingdom at the eve of its downfall.[2]

Already Klein[3] had remarked that there are points of contact between Nehemiah 11 and Joshua 15 and 18, because both lists indicate one and the same territory—the land of the tribe of Judah and Benjamin. But Neh. 11.25-36 is not in any sense a copy of the lists of Joshua, since the latter contains and refers to more localities and had a completely different set of numbers. Kellerman believes that the organization of men in Neh. 11.4-19 according to *bāttê 'ābôt* indicates this list's relation to the seventh to sixth centuries BCE. In my view this fact shows that this list belongs to the Achaemenid period, since the concept *bēt 'ābôt* was not yet in circulation in the seventh to sixth century. Kellerman calls the tribal membership in Neh. 11.25-36 an 'anachronism for the fifth century', but this 'anachronism' occurs still later as well (c.f. *m. Ta'an.* 4.5)—thus, there are no grounds to doubt the historicity of Neh. 11.25-36.[4]

The evidence of Table 4 shows that the growth of the community after 458/457 is matched by a corresponding expansion of the cities occupied by community members, mainly in southern Judah.

Territory	Before 458/457	After 458/457	
	Cities	Cities	Cities Mentioned for the First Time
Judah	3	21	20
Benjamin	16	23	11
Total	19	44	31

Table 4

1. Meyer, *Entstehung*, pp. 105-107; G. von Rad, *Das Geschichtsbild des chronistischen Werkes* (BWANT, IV/3; Stuttgart ,1930), pp. 21-24.

2. U. Kellermann, 'Die Listen in Nehemia 11: Eine Dokumentation aus den letzten Jahren des Reiches Juda?', *ZDPV* 82 (1966), pp. 209-27.

3. Klein, *Land of Judah*, pp. 5-7.

4. Kellermann, 'Die Listen', pp. 209-27.

In this table, only the cities mentioned in the Old Testament are counted, although archaeological and epigraphic data allow one to surmise that community members were also in other cities not mentioned in the Old Testament. Therefore it is necessary to try to clarify the criteria for deciding that a settlement which is neither mentioned in the Old Testament, nor identified with an Old Testament locality, can be recognized as a dwelling place of community members.

Stern[1] separated two cultural zones in Palestine of the Achaemenid period. The first zone encompassed the highlands of Judah and some of Transjordan, whose 'eastern culture' united pre-exilic local traditions with influences coming from Assyria, Babylonia, Egypt and Persia. The second zone, suggested as 'western culture', consisted of mainly the Phoenicians and was strongly influenced by the impact of Hellenism. This latter zone included the coastal plain, Galilee, and part of Samaria. The fact that the zone of the 'eastern culture' corresponds to the area of settlement by the community tempts one to consider all of the settlements of 'eastern culture' as potentially settled by members of the community. But it is obvious that this 'eastern culture' already existed in Babylonian Judah—that is, before the establishment of the citizen–temple community. Secondly, the 'eastern culture' zone also includes areas of Transjordan where there was no mass of community settlers. At the same time, community members were found in the Shephelah, which belonged to the 'western culture' zone. In order to characterize a settlement as a place where community members were found, the qualifications cited by Stern (the 'eastern culture' and its characteristics) must be strengthened by means of Old Testament texts and epigraphic data.

With the help of such criteria one can establish the following additions to the settlement patterns of the community in the second half of the fifth century BCE. In the first region, we can add Gitaim, Zeboim and Neballat to the three cities mentioned before 458/457; in the second region we can add Mizpah, Hazor, Ananiah, Bet-Hakerem and Tekoa to the 15 cities before 458/457; and the third region encompassed a wide area in the second half of the fifth century—mentioned as *hakkikkār* in Neh. 3.22, and Old Testament sources permit a comparison of the toponyms *hakkikkār* (e.g. Gen. 13.12;

1. Stern, *Land of Israel*, pp. 114-23.

19.17) and *kikkar hayyardēn* (Gen. 13.10; 1 Kgs 7.46), thus permitting the conclusion that these toponyms indicate the area of the Jordan Valley from Sukkot to the Dead Sea and the Western bank of this sea. In the second half of the fifth century, we find settled community members not only in Jericho, but also *bêt haggilgāl* (Neh. 12.29) and Engedi, where a seal bearing the name Uriah[1] was found, a name that is widely attested in the community.

Although the number of cities grew and the borders of the regions expanded, they remained isolated from each other, as well as from the newly built regions after 458/457.

The fourth region consists of seven cities mentioned in the Old Testament (Senu'ah, Keilah, Zarah, Jarmut, Adullam, Lachish and Azeqah), to which can perhaps be added the settlements of the Persian era in *Tell el-Rumeiliyeh*, Gezer and others.[2] The fifth region encompassed cities mentioned in the Old Testament (Bet-Zur and Kiriath-Ha-'arba' = Hebron). The sixth region consists of ten cities mentioned in the Old Testament (Dibon = Dimon, Kabzeel = Yekabzeel, Jeshua, Molada, Beit-Palet, Hazar-Shual, Beer-Sheba, Ziklag, Mechona and Ein-Rimon) and also Arad, where ostraca mentioning postexilic *bāttê 'ābôt* have been found.[3]

In the course of the sixth to fourth centuries one can observe a steady and even growth of community members, community cities, and community regions. This is clarified by means of a comparison:

	Before 458/457			After 458/457		
	a*	b*	c*	a*	b*	c*
Absolute Numbers	42,360	19	3	150,000	48+2**	6
Growth	1%	1%	1%	3.6%	2.6%	2%

* a = community members, b = cities, c = regions.

** From the dwelling places of community members not stated in the Old Testament, only Arad and Engedi can be mentioned with certainty at this time.

Table 5

1. B. Mazar and I. Dunayevsky, 'Survey of the Fourth and Fifth Excavations of En-Gedi' [Hebrew], *Yediot* 30 (1966), pp. 3-4, 183.

2. N. Avigad, 'Bet-Šemeš', *EB*, II, pp. 110-18; H.D. Lance, 'Gezer in the Land and History', *BA* 30 (1967), pp. 46; W.G. Dever, 'Gezer', *IEJ* 19 (1969), pp. 241-43.

3. Y. Aharoni, 'Tel Arad', *IEJ* 15 (1965), pp. 250-51.

Despite the undeniable growth of the number of members and the expansion of the settlement area, there were also people within the areas who were not members of the community, that is 'the powerful' of Tekoa (Neh. 3.5) and other examples. On the other hand, not all community members lived inside the six regions. In the report about the plots of the opposition to the community, Nehemiah mentions the *y*^{e}*hûdîm*, who live near them (enemies of the community) (Neh. 4.6), while in the count of those fed by Nehemiah there is also mentioned 'those who come to us who were from the *gôyim* who were around us' (Neh. 5.17). With this, then, it must be observed that the concept *y*^{e}*hûdîm*, in the second half of the fifth century BCE was the preferred self-designation of the community members, while the concept *gôyim* indicated ethnically foreign, non-Yahwistic Palestinians. If one also observes that Hebron[1] and Lachish,[2] also settled by community members, nevertheless belonged to Edomite territory, the inevitable conclusion is that a certain number of community members were also settled outside of the so-called 'community lands'. All that has been said argues against the identification of Judah with the citizen–temple community in the Persian period. As the community members were only a part of the population of Judah (20–70%) and the regions settled by them did not appear to be a conclusive unity, it is more precisely correct to speak of the citizen–temple community in the land of Judah (until the middle of the fifth century) or in the Persian province of Judah (second half of the fifth century BCE). Nevertheless in the course of later development, mainly in the first half of the fourth century, the citizen–temple community and the province of Judah also drew together more and more. Questions that are worth considering, such as relations of property and production, city and *'am hā'āreṣ* must be studied either in the context of the citizen–temple community or outside this socio-political organism in Achaemenid Palestine.

1. E. Mader, *Mambre: Die Ergebnisse der Ausgrabungen im heiligen Bezirk Ramet el-Halil in Südpalästina 1928–1938* (Freiburg i.B., 1957), pp. 206-208.

2. Y. Aharoni, 'Trial Excavation in the "Solar Shrine" at Lachish', *IEJ* 18 (1968), pp. 157-64.

Chapter 3

THE *Bêt 'Ābôt* IN THE SIXTH TO FOURTH CENTURIES BCE

In his inventory of terminology unique to the Priestly Writing (P), Driver[1] mentioned the term *bêt 'ābôt* and its equivalent, *'ābôt*. A further investigation of the use and distribution of this term in the different levels of the Old Testament reveals that *bêt 'ābôt* or *'ābôt* is dominant in the postexilic parts of the Old Testament, while in the pre-exilic parts, the term *bêt 'āb* is characteristic. This conclusion can be proven by comparing the appearance of the terms throughout the Deuteronomistic and Chronicler's historical works, and also Ezra–Nehemiah:

	Joshua–2 Kings	1–2 Chronicles	Ezra–Neh.
bêt 'ābôt	1	24	4
'ābôt	5	22	15
bêt 'āb	35	10	1

Table 1

This table shows that the terms *bêt 'ābôt*/*'ābôt* are characteristic for Old Testament terminology mainly during the Achaemenid period (sixth to fourth century BCE). It can be explicity pointed out that the Chronicler also uses this term whenever his Deuteronomic reference material is not before him. Thus, for example, the Chronicler repeats, nearly word for word, the Deuteronomic historian's description of the conspiracy of Jehoiada (2 Kgs 11.4-20). However, he also refers to the 'leaders of the *'ābôt*' (2 Chron. 23.2) as participants in this conspiracy although this is not mentioned in the Deuteronomic material. This and similar examples allow one to conclude that the term under consideration is unique to the postexilic period.

It should be pointed out that this term is common in the late

1. S.R. Driver, *An Introduction to the Literature of the Old Testament* (Edinburgh, 1909), p. 133.

literature.[1] The term also occurs in an inventory in M.Ta'anit 4.5, enumerating collectives of the Achaemenid period—Arah, Parosh, Pahat-Moab for example—which Klein[2] dates in the first century BCE, also recognizing its authenticity. Liver,[3] who doubted the authenticity of the list, nevertheless granted that it described historical realities of the postexilic period. Finally, it must also be observed that the term *'ābôt* appears in the Qumran writings (1QSa 1.16, 24, 25; 1QM 2.1, 3, 7) where a possible social unity within the community is identified. It is reasonable to propose that the terms *bêt 'ābôt/'ābôt* refer to an actual social institution in the postexilic period.

The interpretation of the terms *bêt 'ābôt/'ābôt* that are suggested in the relevant literature can be summarized and listed as follows:

1. The *bêt 'ābôt* is a 'clan' (extended kin group) (Amusin, Bühl, Kittel, Klausner, Liver, Meyer, Zucker, etc.).[4]
2. The *bêt 'ābôt* is a family, or band of families (de Vaux, Galling, Noth, Pedersen, etc.).[5]
3. The *bêt 'ābôt* is a local community structure (Mowinckel).[6]

The existence of such basically different viewpoints proves that the meaning of the *bêt 'ābôt* is still not clear and thus justifies an attempt to arrive at a detailed and more complete understanding of this problem.

1. H. Kreissig, *Die sozialen Zusammenhänge des judäischen Krieges* (Berlin, 1970), p. 55.

2. Sh. Klein, 'The Rollbook of Geneaologies Found in Jerusalem' [Hebrew], *Zion* IV (1939), pp. 31-32.

3. J. Liver, *The History of the House of David, from the Destruction of the State of Judah to the Destruction of the Second Temple* [Hebrew] (Jerusalem, 1959), p. 24.

4. J.D. Amusin, 'People of the Land' [Russian], *VDI* 2 (1955), p. 29; F. Bühl, *Die sozialen Verhältnisse der Israeliten* (Berlin, 1899), p. 37; J. Klausner, 'The History of the Second Temple I' [Hebrew] (Jerusalem, 1954), pp. 190-91; J. Liver, *The Time of Ezra and Nehemiah* [Hebrew] (Jerusalem, 1953), pp. 10-11; E. Meyer, *Die Entstehung des Judentums* (Halle, 1896), pp. 134-35; H. Zucker, *Studien zur jüdischen Selbstverwaltung im Altertum* (Berlin, 1936), pp. 9-14.

5. R. de Vaux, *Les institutions de l'Ancien Testament*, I (Paris, 1958), p. 22; M. Noth, *Die Welt des Alten Testaments* (Berlin, 1957), p. 55; K. Galling, *Studien zur Geschichte Israels im persischen Zeitalter* (Tübingen, 1964), p. 96; J. Pedersen, *Israel: Its Life and Culture*, I-II (Oxford, 1926), pp. 46-48.

6. S. Mowinckel, *Studien zu dem Buche Ezra–Nehemia,* I (Oslo, 1964), pp. 71-91.

Although the archaeological and epigraphical discoveries of the last decades have greatly expanded the sources available for the study of Judah in the Achaemenid period, the Old Testament books of Ezra–Nehemiah are still our main source. In Ezra–Nehemiah, the terms *bêt 'ābôt*/*'ābôt* are used 19 times in various contexts. An investigation of the meaning in each case will contribute toward a clarification of the nature of the institution which is indicated.

The *bêt 'ābôt* is mentioned many times in conjunction with the repatriation of the exiles from Mesopotamia. In the description of the first repatriation it is reported that after the publication of the edict of Cyrus, 'the heads of *bêt 'ābôt* of Judah and of Benjamin, the priests and the Levites rose up...' (Ezra 1.5). With regard to the three lay-collectives, it is said 'and these returnees...could not prove that their *bêt 'ābôt* and ancestry were of Israelite origin...' and because of this, they were (temporarily) excluded from the postexilic community (Neh. 7.61-62; Ezra 2.59-60).[1] Perhaps one is justified in assuming that the remaining returnee-collectives, which were refered to in a manner similar to the three excluded groups, according to the formula 'sons of X', could indicate that their *bêt 'ābôt* were indeed *bêt 'ābôt*. Accordingly, the 'introduction' of the authentic[2] returnee list in Ezra 8.1-14, states: 'And these are the heads of their *'ābôt*...' In these four texts, the term *bêt 'ābôt* refers to a lay collective of the returnees.

In three places, the leaders of the *'ābôt* are mentioned as those who bring gifts for the Jerusalem temple. Galling,[3] who argues for the credibility of this description, points out the crucial differences in the parallel written records of the gifts and their bearers:

> A certain number of heads of the *'ābôt* contributed to the work, the *tiršātā* contributed...to the fund...and heads of the *'ābôt* gave...to the work fund...(Neh.7.69-71)

> A certain number of heads of the *'ābôt* made voluntary offerings for the Temple of God, for its rebuilding on its site... (Ezra 2.68)

In Ezra 2.68 the gifts are specifically for the rebuilding of the temple,

1. In my opinion Neh. 7.7-69 is the original place of the list, and this is its early form.

2. The objections of Mowinckel (*Studien*, I, pp. 116-23) and Kellermann ('Erwägungen zum Esragesetz', *ZAW* 80 [1968], pp. 55-56) against the authenticity of the list are not convincing.

3. Galling, *Studien*, pp. 101-105.

while in Neh. 7.70-71 they were brought for the 'work', the 'fund' and the 'fund of the work'. The word *m*^{e}*lā'kâ* is often used as a technical term for cultic functions (e.g. 1 Chron. 26.30; 28.13; Neh. 11.22; 13.10),[1] while the term *'ōṣār* sometimes indicates the treasury or the storehouse of the Jerusalem temple. If one keeps in mind that in Neh. 7.70-71 the *tiršātā* is mentioned among the donors, and that this title was used only for Nehemiah (e.g. Neh. 8.9; 10.2) and one other unnamed person (Ezra 2.63 = Neh. 7.65) who was active in the community before 458/7, the conclusion can be drawn that in the original list (Neh. 7), the head of the *'ābôt* offered gifts for the completed temple. This means that the *'ābôt* were collectives in the emergent citizen–temple community in Judah.

In the year 520 BCE, in order to ask permission to participate in the temple reconstruction, the 'people of the land' (mainly the Samaritans), directed their request to 'Zerubabel and heads of the *'ābôt*' (Ezra 4.2) and also received from them a refusal (v. 3). In the year 458/7 BCE, the 'heads of the *'ābôt*' (Ezra 10.16) played a decisive role in the break-up of mixed marriages. The objections raised against the credibility of the list in Ezra 10.18-44 by Kellerman[2] and Mowinckel[3] are not convincing. On the basis of his assumption that the Ezra story belongs to the literary category of a pious historical tale, a pious fictionalization about an ideal saint—Ezra—in an ideal model-community,[4] Mowinckel denies the authenticity of the list of families, since it contradicts the sense and content of such a novella. But Mowinckel's position with regard to the literary form of the Ezra story is quite controversial.[5] Furthermore, it is important to take into account the various connections between the returnees and different ethnic groups that lived in Palestine, as well as the tendency, in relation to the previous point, of the citizen–temple community itself

1. W. Baudissin, *Die Geschichte des alttestamentlichen Priestertums* (Leipzig, 1889), pp. 160ff.

2. Kellermann, *Erwägungen*, pp. 55-56.

3. Mowinckel, *Studien*, pp. 124-30.

4. S. Mowinckel, '*Ich* und *Er* in der Ezrageschichte', *Verbannung und Heimkehr: Beiträge zur Geschichte und Theologie Israels im 6. und 5. Jahrhundert v. Chr.* (Tübingen, 1961), pp. 230-32; and *Studien zu dem Buche Ezra–Nehemia*, III (Oslo, 1965), pp. 70-74.

5. J. Weinberg, Review of *Verbannung und Heimkehr: Beiträge zur Geschichte und Theologie Israels im 6. und 5. Jahrhundert v. Chr. W. Rudolph zum 70. Geburtstage dargebracht*, *VDI* 2 (1968), pp. 162-63.

toward a conscious isolationism. The fact that only collectives from the list in Neh. 7 = Ezra 2 are mentioned in the inventory of the mixed marriages speaks for the credibility of Ezra 10.8-44 since it deals with a 'delinquency' of the members of the citizen–temple community.

If one keeps in mind that in Nehemiah the *bāttê 'ābôt* (this form does not occur, but will herein indicate plural) of the priests are often mentioned (11.13; 12.22), and more seldom the Levites (12.13), this further verifies the conclusion that the *bêt 'ābôt* was a social institution; a collective within the citizen–temple community of the sixth to fourth century BCE.

In order to clarify the meaning of the *bêt 'ābôt*, we can consider first all the evidence about the 17 lay *bêt 'ābôt* (Neh. 7.8-24–Ezra 2.3-19). This list, as I have elsewhere suggested,[1] is an inventory of the collectives which compose the citizen–temple community up to the year 458/7 BCE. The lay *bāttê 'ābôt*, the 'men of the people of Israel', encompass 16,722/15,520 persons, or 54.9/53.2% of the members of the community.

	Name	Quantity of Men
1	Par'osh	2172
2	Shephatiah	372
3	Araḥ	652/775*
4	Paḥat-Moab	2818/2812
5	'Elam	1254
6	Zattu'	845/945
7	Zakkai	760
8	Binnui/Bani	648/642
9	Bebai	628/623
10	'Azgad	2322/1222
11	Adoniqam	667/666
12	Bigwai	2067/2056
13	'Adin	655/454
14	'Aṭer	98
15	Ḥashum	328/223
16	Beṣai	324/323
17	Ḥariph/Jora	112

* The first number is from Neh. 7, the second from Ezra 2.

Table 2

1. J.P. Weinberg, 'Demographische Notizen zur Geschichte der nachexilischen Gemeinde in Juda', *Klio* 54 (1972), pp. 51-52.

Before we consider the data more carefully, it is worth adding that only the numbers of mature men in the *bāttê 'ābôt* are listed. Not only is this in keeping with the general rule of Old Testament demographic statistics,[1] but it is also proved by a formula that we find repeated in Ezra 8: 'and with him (named persons) x (number of men)'. The dates in Table 2 prove that most of the *bāttê 'ābôt* had of a number of men up to 1000 (77.8%). This average contradicts the supposition that the *bêt 'ābôt* was a family, and enables a comparison of the Old Testament *bêt 'ābôt* with the large agnatic group of ancient Iran, which consisted of 600 mature men.[2]

Meyer[3] had already commented that in the inventory of lay *bāttê 'ābôt*, a conscious order of ranking is recognizable, but he did not consider this in relation to the numbers within the collectives. The data in Table 2 reveals that of the five smallest *bāttê 'ābôt* (with a membership of up to 400), four collectives (nos. 14–17) are listed as last in the inventory, while almost all *bāttê 'ābôt* with an average quantity of members (up to 1000) are placed in the middle of the inventory (nos. 6–9, 11, 13). A strict rank-ordering is not clear, and it is possible to assume that the place of a *bêt 'ābôt* in the inventory is a measure of its influence and placement in the community, which is partially related to its quantitative circumstances.[4]

The *bêt 'ābôt* had a complicated inner structure, which is revealed by the full designation of the largest collective (no. 4): 'The sons of Paḥat-Moab, of the sons of Jeshua and Joab...'

The preposition *lamed* is often used in the Old Testament, in order to express belonging, or the concept of the genitive. As the words *ben* (son) and *bāyit* (house) are frequently used as synonyms for blood-relations,[5] the designation of number 4 can be reconstructed as, 'the sons of Paḥat-Moab, belonging to the house of Jeshua and Joab' (cf. Neh. 7.39; Ezra 2.36). That means the *bêt 'ābôt* Pahat-Moab was

1. G.E. Mendenhall, 'The Census List in Numbers 1 and 26', *JBL* 27 (1958), pp. 52-66.

2. A.G. Perichanian, 'Agnatic Groups in Ancient Iran' [Russian], *VDI* 3 (1968), pp. 37.

3. Meyer, *Entstehung*, pp. 154-56.

4. An analogous appearance is also in Arrapcha: N.B. Jankovskaja, 'On the discussion about the Clan- and Rural-Community in the Ancient East' [Russian], *VDI* I (1963), p. 181.

5. Sh. Talmon, 'Synonymous Readings in the Textual Traditions of the Old Testament', *Scripta Hierosolymitana* 8 (1961), p. 346.

a segment of the house of Jeshua and Joab, from which in the years c. 458/57 BCE another segment 'the sons of Joab' broke off (Ezra 8.9).

The designation of the smallest of the 17 collectives, 'the sons of 'Ater from the (house of) Hezekiah' (no. 14), refers as well to the complicated inner structure of the *bêt 'ābôt*. The strikingly small number of its members (only 98 men) reveals that the *bêt 'ābôt* under examination was a segment of a larger unity, the house of Hezekiah. Such segments of the larger *bāttê 'ābôt* were also the majority (75%) of the collectives of the returnees in the year 458/457 BCE. This is indicated not only by the heading of the lists of these returnees (Ezra 8.1) but also by the often repeated formula; 'from (*min*) the sons of Z (the enumeration of a *bêt 'ābôt* mentioned in Neh. 7–Ezra 2) X, son of Y, and with him (number of men)'. This formula used the preposition *min*, which in its rootmeaning expresses separation or partitioning, and occurs in a partitive manner in the Old Testament. The number of the men in such segments varies, according to Ezra 8, from 50 to 218, but involves, in the majority of cases, some 70 men. In the fourth stratum of Engedi (fifth century BCE) a large construction (550 m^2) with 23 rooms was discovered where 'a very large family was resident...'[1] For the *bêt 'ābôt* of the sixth to fourth century BCE, a carefully outlined and important family tree is recognizable. This explains the richness of the genealogies in the Old Testament and apocryphal works of the postexilic era, the appearance of the term *hityaḥēś*[2] and the occurrence of special genealogies (Neh. 7.5) which, as M. Ta'anit 4.5 proves, is also present in later periods. The genealogy was no minor formality but was an important attribute of the *bêt 'ābôt*, and its absence could provide either a reason (or a pretext) for the exclusion of a collective from the citizen–temple community.

Neh. 11.4	Neh. 11.5	Neh. 11.12	Neh. 11.13
Athaya	Ma'aseiah	Adaiah	Amashsai
Uzziah	Baruch	Jeroham	Azar'el
Zechariah	*Kolhozeh*	Pelahiah	Achzai
Amariah	Hazaiah	Amsi	Meshillemoth
Shephatiah	Adaiah	Zechariah	*Immer*
Mahalal'el	Jojarib	*Pashhur*	
	Zechariah	Malkariah	

Table 3

1. B. Mazar and I. Dunayevsky, 'Eingeddi', *IEJ* 15 (1965), pp. 258-59.
2. J. Liver, 'Geneaology' [Hebrew], *EB*, III, pp. 663-67.

In the authentic list[1] in Neh. 11.4ff., more genealogies of the fifth century BCE are mentioned, which enables us to take a look at the construction and meaning of these family trees.

In these, as in other genealogies, the names of the fifth or the sixth (more seldom the third) member of the family tree (in the table in italics) correspond to the names of known lay or priestly collectives of the postexilic era. If it can be assumed that these lines of the genealogy include real persons of the collective,[2] then they lived 90 to 150–180 years before the second half of the fifth century BCE, that is between the second half of the sixth century and the end of the seventh century BCE. Pashhur son of Malkariah (Jer. 21.1; 38.1) and Pashhur, son of Immer (Jer. 20.1ff.) lived in this time. It can be assumed that the genealogies of the postexilic *bêt 'ābôt* encompassed an average of three to six generations beginning with the ancestor after whom the collective is named. Since a similar phenomenon appears in the citizen–temple community of Seleucid Uruk, in Palmyra in the second to third century BCE, and in other places,[3] the conclusion appears to be that the *bêt 'ābôt* is a collection of many families related either by being descendants of three or six generations of an ancestor or through relationship (whether real or fictional) with him.

Meyer[4] suggested that the full name of a free man also indicated the name of his collective, and that in the formula 'X son of Y, son of Z', the last names are often the name of the collective. Mowinckel[5] disagreed, suggesting the view that in the three-part formula the third name is that of the actual grandfather. An overview of the available data in Ezra–Nehemiah speaks for Meyer's view. If in day-to-day affairs the member of the citizen–temple community is indicated only by his name and his father's name, so on official or solemn occasions the name of the *bêt 'ābôt* is also used, for example, 'of the sons of Adin, Ebed, son of Jonathan' (Ezra 8.6). This three-part formula is

1. Sh. Klein, *Land of Judah*, pp. 5-7.
2. A. Malamat, 'King Lists of the Old Babylonian Period and Biblical Genealogies', *JAOS* 88 (1968), pp. 163-73.
3. G.Ch. Sarkisian, 'Self-Governing Towns in Seleucid Babylonia' [Russian], *VDI* 1 (1965), pp. 71-73.
4. Meyer, *Entstehung*, pp. 138-40.
5. Mowinckel, *Studien*, I, pp. 81-84.

repeated in the enumeration of the participants in the building of the Jerusalem wall, for example, 'Meremoth, son of Uriah, son of Hakkoṣ' (Neh. 3.4). In this list a two-part name formula is also used in which the second part indicates the name of the *bêt 'ābôt*, for example 'Hashub, son of Pahat-Moab' (v. 11). The mention of the agnatic group as a component of the proper name is a frequent occurrence in the ancient Near East,[1] although in some cases the third name in the three-part formula can also be the name of the actual grandfather.

Old Testament and epigraphic data prove that the members of the *bêt 'ābôt* indicated their membership with the term *ben* (son; Neh. 7 = Ezra 2; Ezra 8, etc.). This concept indicates the membership of an individual to an ethnic, blood-related and professional community.[2] The term *'āḥ* (brother) indicated not only the real brother, but all male members of the *bêt 'ābôt* (Neh. 11.12-13) and one can agree with Freiman[3] when he refers to the *bêt 'ābôt* as a 'unity of brothers'. Also in the house-community of the Near East until the middle of the second millennium BCE, the concept 'brother' designates not only the real brother, but can also mean all agnatic members of the community in question.[4]

In this term of membership of the *bêt 'ābôt*, the principle of solidarity is revealed, as well as in the use of the *ge'ullâ* (Ruth 4.9-10) in the right of first purchase, redemption property and in the latent law of inheritance. All these solidarity principles flow together in the property relations of the *bêt 'ābôt*. I have dealt with this question in another work,[5] so it is only necessary to point to the most important conclusions; the majority of the lands of the citizen–temple community were common property of the *bêt 'ābôt*, which was divided in parcels, occupied in turn by the families. This dominant communal land formed the economic basis of the *bêt 'ābôt*, and was the most important unifying factor which sustained the inner unity and relative stability of the *bêt 'ābôt*.

For that reason, the heads (*rā'šîm*) of the *bāttê 'ābôt* were very powerful and played an important role in the life of the citizen–temple

1. Perichanian, *Agnatic Groups*, p. 40ff.
2. G. Brin, 'On the Title: Son of the King' [Hebrew], *Leš* 31(1967), pp. 93-96.
3. A.Ch. Freiman, 'Brother and Sister' [Hebrew], *EB*, I, pp. 191-93.
4. I.M. Diakanoff, 'Economic Problems: On the Stucture of Near Eastern Society to the Middle of the 2nd Millenium BCE' [Russian], *VDI* 3 (1968), pp. 10ff.
5. Weinberg, 'Agrarverhältnisse', pp. 1-4.

community and the individual collectives. The 'heads of the *'ābôt* from their *bêt 'ābôt*' (Ezra 10.16) participated in an active manner in the intricate and difficult divorce of the mixed marriages. The rebuilding of the walls of Jerusalem was an undertaking that required time and power, and one in which 'the people' (Neh. 4.4,7,16) participated. Nevertheless, only the heads of the Hakkoṣides, the Paḥat-Moabians and other *bāttê 'ābôt* were counted among the builders. It is highly probable that each of the heads that are mentioned led a working group from among the members of his *bêt 'ābôt*. In any case, the head of the *'ābôt* could intervene in the lives of the constituent families and in certain cases had authority over the working-power of the collective which he led.

While I have revealed the real existence of the *bêt 'ābôt* in the sixth to fourth centuries, and have shown its most notable aspects, the question of its nature is not yet clear. It is worthwhile discovering the historical root of the postexilic *bêt 'ābôt*. This question has already been raised in the scholarly literature. The most prominent exponents of opposite standpoints are Meyer,[1] who suggested that the majority of the postexilic *bāttê 'ābôt* were rooted in the pre-exilic Judaean society, while Mowinckel[2] was convinced that all the *bāttê 'ābôt* were from the exilic or postexilic era. For the solution of this question both scholars used mainly onomastic materials of the sixth to fourth centuries BCE.

The following attempt toward a new solution to this old question is based on an evaluation of the onomastic materials, the designation of the *bāttê 'ābôt* and the names of its members. Since a detailed discussion of methodology is not possible, only the most important points will be mentioned:

1. My task is to confirm which of the lay *bāttê 'ābôt* of the sixth to fourth centuries BCE are rooted in the pre-exilic milieu, and to determine the essence of this milieu, as well as to reveal those *bāttê 'ābôt* to be without a pre-exilic root.

2. As part of the solution to this task, the relevant onomastic materials were referred to and the character of the oft-discussed Israelite naming-structures were reviewed, for example, the availability of certain name-types, the spread of certain names or name-types within different social or

1. Meyer, *Entstehung*, pp. 156-61.
2. Mowinckel, *Studien*, I, pp. 79-81.

professional circles as well as local unities, the practice of papponomy, the naming of many *bāttê 'ābôt* after real persons, etc.

3. The names of all lay *bāttê 'ābôt*, and the personal names of their members, were examined in the Old Testament and in epigraphic material in order arrive at one of four possible options: a) there is not enough data available to determine the root of the *bêt 'ābôt*; b) the *bêt 'ābôt* is *possibly* rooted in the pre- or exilic/postexilic milieu; c) the *bêt 'ābôt* is rooted in the pre-exilic milieu; d) the *bêt 'ābôt* is rooted in the milieu of the exilic or early postexilic time.

4. The 'milieu', in this connection, merely means the area, the territory and the social or professional circle within which the root of the corresponding *bêt 'ābôt* is to be sought.

In the history of the citizen–temple community, two basically different developmental stages can be determined, which are differentiated by the year 458/457 BCE. Until 458/7, we can speak of the emergent community, while after 458/7, we refer to the fully developed community.[1] This periodization should correspond also to the presentation of the onomastic data.

For the time before the year 458/457 BCE, we know of the earlier mentioned seventeen *bāttê 'ābôt* (Table 2) as well as the three collectives originally excluded from the community (who were, of course, later re-admitted according to Neh. 7.61-62 = Ezra 2.59-60: Delaiah, Tobiah, and Neqoda). We have no information about one *bêt 'ābôt* (no. 20) which would allow any certainty about its provenance (option a). With regard to the remaining 19 *bāttê 'ābôt*, nine (47%) are rooted in the pre-exilic, Judaean milieu (option c), while in reference to an other nine (47%) a pre-exilic or exilic/postexilic origin is possible (option b), and one *bêt 'ābôt* is to be certainly located in the exilic or early postexilic period (option d). All nine *bāttê 'ābôt* of pre-exilic origin are genetically related to residents of the Judaean state, mainly in southern areas; however four or five collectives are possibly connected with the Davidides.

After 458/7 BCE there appear nine *bāttê 'ābôt*, which are mentioned in different lists (Table 4).

1. Weinberg, 'Demographische Notizen', p. 54.

Of the twelve *bāttê 'ābôt* of this group, one can determine a pre-exilic root for nine (option c); however, for the remaining three (25%) a pre-exilic source is not out of the question (option b).

	Name	Source		Name	Source
21*	David	Ezra 8.2	27	Hur	Neh. 3.9
22	Shehaniah	Ezra 8.5	28	Hallohesh	Neh. 3.12
23	Shelomith	Ezra 8.10	29	Rehab	Neh. 3.14
24	Hakaliah	Neh. 1.1	30	Kol-hoze	Neh. 3.15
25	Ba'ana	Neh. 3.4	31	Azbuk	Neh. 3.16
26	Meshezabel	Neh. 3.4	32	Ananiah	Neh. 3.23

* The numeration is continuing from Table 2, above.

Table 4

The collected results of this onomastic investigation are gathered together in Table 5:

Option of the *bāttê 'ābôt*		*bāttê 'ābôt* of sixth to fourth centuries BCE	
	Milieu	Before 458/457	After 458/457
Pre-exilic	Judaean	9 (47%)	9 (75%)
	Including Davidic	5	1
Pre- or postexilic	-	9 (47%)	3 (25%)
Exilic or postexilic	-	1 (6%)	-

Table 5

The data of the table reveal that the majority of the lay *bāttê 'ābôt* of the sixth to fourth centuries BCE had a pre-exilic root, and were genetically related with the population of Judah in the first half of the first millennium BCE.

This conclusion now allows a further question to be raised. To which institution of the pre-exilic era does the postexilic *bêt 'ābôt* relate? The term *bêt 'ābôt* is etymologically cognate to the term *bêt 'āb*, widely attested in the first half of the first millennium. In Josh. 7.16ff where there is given a cross-section of Israelite society at the end of the second millennium to the early first millennium, one finds a tribe, a clan (*mišpāḥâ*) and a *bêt 'āb*, that is, large patriarchal families. The socio-political development of Palestine, particularly the southern area, was a relatively long process. It maintained, therefore, even after the construction of a class society and important state structures of the tribe-clan organization.[1] The clan still played a meaningful role[2]

1. A.M. Gazov-Ginzberg, 'The Struggle between Ethnic Groups (Tribes) for Power in the Israelite Kingdom' [Russian], *PS* 11 (1964), pp. 25-38.

in the social, communal and political life of the eighth century BCE; the system of the property relations that predominated in the first half of the first millennium BCE proves the actual existence of the *mišpāḥâ* Further, Old Testament data suggest that the *bêt 'ābôt* still actively existed and functioned (Isa. 22.23; Jer. 12.6, etc.) in the seventh to sixth centuries BCE. In relation to this it should be observed that the *bêt 'ābôt* of the Rechabites (Table 4, no. 29) is mentioned at the end of the seventh century BCE as 'house of Rechabites', with a head of the house, and 'his brothers and all their sons' (Jer. 25.3-4).[1] The *bêt 'ābôt* of the Achaemenid era is found in genetic relationship with the *mišpāḥâ* or *bêt 'āb* of the pre-exilic society. In relation to this, however, one must not be simplistic and see the *bêt 'ābôt* as merely a direct development of the pre-exilic institutions, since between the two, the destruction of the Judaean state occured with its repeated deportations which concerned mainly the southern part of Judah. Through this catastrophe, many *mišpāḥôt* and *bāttê 'ābôt* were destroyed or dispersed. But in the unique situation of the exile and the return, the necessity of consolidation among the exiles and returnees furthered the formation of a new social construction from the pieces of pre-exilic institutions—the *bāttê 'ābôt* of the sixth to fourth centuries BCE.

The *bêt 'ābôt* of the Achaemenid era is an agnatic band which came into existence in the peculiar situation of the exile and repatriation, and which unified a number of families that were related (either genuinely or fictionally). The essential characteristics of the *bêt 'ābôt* are a large quantitative composition and a complicated inner structure, an obligatory genealogy and inclusion of the name of the *bêt 'ābôt* in the full name of each of its members and a conscious solidarity based on communal ownership of lands. All of these aspects point to a typological similarity of the *bêt 'ābôt* with the old Near Eastern agnatic band, which is often called a 'house-community'.[2] Since we also meet the *bêt 'ābôt* among other social and professional groups of the community as well (mainly among the priests), it must be the case that this large agnatic unity was the basic structural unit of the citizen-temple community of the sixth to fourth centuries BCE.

2. I.S. Shiffman, 'The Agrarian System in Palestine in the First Half of the 1st Millenium BCE' [Russian], *VDI* 4 (1965), pp. 33ff.

1. Sh. Abramsky, 'The Rechabite Genealogy and Social Structure' [Hebrew], *E-I* 8 (1967), pp. 255-58.

2. Diakanoff, 'Economic Problems', p. 7.

Chapter 4

THE *'Am Hā'āreṣ* OF THE SIXTH TO FOURTH CENTURIES BCE

I

On the treacherous path of the ancient historian, there is many a Scylla and Charibdis, among which ancient socio-political terminology is especially insidious. Often one and the same term will encompass multifaceted and basically different concepts, and the sense of a word can even evolve to the opposite of its original meaning.

An example of this is the term *'am hā'āreṣ*, which was, for almost 1500 years, one of the most important constituent parts of ancient Hebrew socio-political terminology, and in the course of centuries it indicated basically different social phenomena of the changing society of Palestine. At the end of its semantic evolution, in the Mishnah and in the Talmud, it denoted the poor and uneducated peasants,[1] while in the first half of the first millenium BCE, the *'am hā'āreṣ* was mainly the designation of fully-enfranchised citizens and land owners.[2] How did it go through such a semantic transformation?

In order to answer this question, it is worthwhile turning to the sixth to fourth centuries BCE. The far-reaching events of these three centuries—the breakdown of the Jewish state, the exile and the appearance of the citizen–temple community—brought about important changes in the socio-economic structure which are also reflected in socio-political terminology. It is furthermore interesting that in the voluminous literature about the *'am hā'āreṣ*, the fate of this group in the sixth to fourth centuries is seldom considered.

In order to determine the content of a socio-political term, it is

1. L. Finkelstein, *The Pharisees: The Sociological Background of their Faith*, I (Philadelphia, 1940), pp. 24-37; H. Kreissig, *Die sozialen Zusammenhänge des judäischen Krieges* (Berlin, 1970), pp. 84-86.

2. J.D. Amusin, 'The People of the Land' [Russian], *VDI* 2 (1955), pp. 24-25.

essential to compare it not only with similar terms but also with opposite terms. This is all the more important for a determination of the term, *'am hā'āreṣ* and its use in the sixth to fourth centuries BCE, when the citizen–temple community encompassed only a part of Judah and its residents.[1] In Palestine, there existed still other socio-political structures besides the citizen–temple community in the Achaemenid era. The relationship between this community and the structures belongs among the most important factors which influenced the development and the essence of the postexilic community. Since the term *'am hā'āreṣ* appears in the sources of the sixth to fourth centuries BCE as an indication of one of these structures, and also as a self-designation of the postexilic community, it is worthwhile in the first place to investigate the names used by the citizen–temple community for itself.

II

The names used by the postexilic community itself were recently analyzed by Vogt.[2] Two main objections, however, must be made with regard to his investigation. Vogt is convinced that the postexilic community was, in essence, a religious community,[3] and therefore he sought a religious sense or content to all terms used by the community itself. Besides this, Vogt is of the opinion that the essence and structure of the community in the sixth to fourth centuries BCE did not change, and he believes that the terminology used by the community to identify itself remained constant.

	Group	Before 458/457	After 458/457
1.	'The returnees from exile'	4	-
2.	'Sons of the exile, the exile'	5	2
3.	'Israel'	17	15
4.	'Community, Assembly'	1	9
5.	'People'	13	33
6.	'Judaeans'	8	11
7.	*'am hā'āreṣ*	(see Table 2)	

Table 1

1. J.P. Weinberg, 'Demographische Notizen zur Geschichte der nachexilischen Gemeinde in Juda', *Klio* 54 (1972), pp. 54-58.

2. H.C.M. Vogt, *Studien zur nachexilischen Gemeinde in Esra–Nehemia* (Werl, 1966).

3. Vogt, *Studien*, pp. 157-60.

That these two views are questionable is revealed through a simple enumeration (Table 1) of the most important self-designations and their appearance in Ezra–Nehemiah, with regard to the events before and after 458/457 BCE in the citizen–temple community.

The data of Table 1 indicate essential changes in the use of different self-designations before and after 458/457. To see that these changes were not accidental, it is instructive to observe individual terms and their use.

1. The term 'returnees from the exile' (*hā'ôlîm, habbā'îm, haššābîm miššᵉbî haggôlâ*) designates mainly those who returned from Babylon (e.g. Neh. 7.61 = Ezra 2.59; Ezra 3.8; 6.21). Occasionally there are cases when this term encompasses all members of the emergent citizen–temple community (Neh. 7.6; Ezra 2.1), including not only those who returned, but also a certain number of those inhabitants in Judah who were not deported. This demonstrates the aspiration of the returnees to assert their leading and dominant place in the community. This tendency naturally diminished after 458/457 BCE as the citizen–temple community assimilated an influx from the inhabitants of Judah[1] who were not deported. Correspondingly, the self-designation 'returnees from the exile' began to lose its original significance, and after 458/457 it was not used any longer.

2. What was said with regard to the first term is similar to the case with the term 'sons of the exile' (*bᵉnê haggôlâ*), or 'the exiles' (*haggôlâ*), which was used until 458/457 BCE and denoted only the returnees (e.g. Ezra 6.20; 10.16). After the expansion and consolidation of the community this term also dropped out of use as a self-designation for the community, since it no longer corresponded to the actual constituency of the community.

3. Danell[2] considers the term 'Israel' (*yiśrā'ēl*) in Ezra–Nehemiah as one of many self-designations of the postexilic community, but according to von Rad[3] the character of the postexilic community as a religious community is appropriately expressed through this term.

1. J.P. Weinberg, 'Collectives Named after Localities in Achaemenid Judah' [Russian], *ArOr* 42.4 (1974) pp. 341-53.

2. G.A. Danell, *Studies in the Name Israel in the Old Testament* (Uppsala, 1946), pp. 281-84, 287-91.

3. G. von Rad, *Das Geschichtsbild des chronistischen Werkes* (BWANT, IV/3; Stuttgart, 1930), pp. 19-20.

Vogt[1] supposes that the wide-spread use of this designation implies that the postexilic community saw itself as the entire people consisting of twelve tribes. But it should be clarified that in Ezra–Nehemiah the term 'Israel' appears as (a) a designation for the entire community and (b) a designation of a part of its members. In Ezra–Nehemiah the term 'Israel' frequently denotes the twelve tribes in the time of Moses and Joshua (Ezra 6.17; Neh. 8.1, 14). Therefore we can conclude that 'Israel' was a designation of the entire community which reflected the thoughts and expectations of those people in the citizen–temple community who hoped to restore a structure similar to the so-called amphictyony, which is also called 'Israel' in the Old Testament.[2] In Ezra–Nehemiah, especially after 458/457 BCE (e.g. Ezra 7.7, 10.25, Neh. 11.3) 'Israel' is often used to designate the laymen in the community. Therefore 'Israel' was not the self-designation *par excellence* of the citizen–temple community, but only one of many terms.

4. Several scholars are of the opinion that the terms *qāhāl* and *'ēdâ* were in use relatively late (fourth century BCE), but there are convincing arguments which prove the use of those terms already in the first half of the first millenium BCE and maybe earlier.[3] Some scholars see these words as *terminus technicus* for a cult-community,[4] but Barr[5] proved that *qāhāl* means an 'assembly' or 'group' without a necessarily religious character. Malamat[6] suggests that *qāhāl* was a popular assembly in the Judaean state, while in the opinion of Noth and Buccellati[7] this term, as well as the word *'ēdâ*, describes the amphictyony in the fourteenth to twelfth centuries BCE and their leading structure. In this latter meaning, that is, as designations for one of the leading institutions in the system of self-government of the

1. Vogt, *Studien*, pp. 47-65.

2. M. Noth, *Das System der zwölf Stämme Israels* (BWANT, IV/1; Stuttgart, 1930), pp. 90-108. I am aware that Noth's theory is now under severe criticism.

3. S.R. Driver, *An Introduction to the Literature of the Old Testament* (Edinburgh, 1909), p. 133; E. Urbach, 'Key-Words in the Priestly Tora' [Hebrew] (PHLHB, 2; 1956), pp. 37-38; Noth, *Das System*, p. 102.

4. S. Mowinckel, *Studien zu dem Buche Ezra–Nehemia*, I (Oslo, 1964), pp. 85-90; von Rad, *Das Geschichtsbild*, pp. 44-45; Vogt, *Studien*, pp. 90-99, 13.

5. J. Barr, *The Semantics of Biblical Language* (London, 1962), pp. 120-28.

6. A. Malamat, 'Organs of Statecraft in the Israelite Monarchy', *BA* 28 (1965), pp. 37-38.

7. Noth, *Das System*, p. 102; G. Buccellati, *Cities and Nations of Ancient Syria* (Rome, 1967), p. 102.

citizen–temple community, these terms are often used after 458/457 BCE.

5. Pedersen and Speiser[1] are of the opinion that the term *'am* (people, nation) mainly with an article or in a construct state, signified a community consolidated on a real or fictitious blood relationship. Vogt[2] suggested that in Ezra–Nehemiah the term 'people' expresses mainly the union of the community with Yahweh in the sense of 'the people of Yahweh'. In response to Vogt's opinion, it must be noted that only Ezra 1.3 can be interpreted as 'the people of Yahweh', while in all the other cases *'am* either was used to describe the entirety of the community members (Ezra 3.11, 7.25) or the non-priestly part of the community (Neh. 7.72 = Ezra 2.70, Ezra 7.16), but without any hint of a necessarily religious interpretation. After 458/457 BCE the term *'am* described mainly the ordinary members of the community in contrast to the top (Neh. 10.29, 35; 12.20). At that time the term 'people' was only seldom used to signify the entire community, because a more exact self-designation already existed.

6. In the description of the events before 458/458 BCE the term 'Judaean' (*y^{e}hûdîm*) is mentioned only in Ezra 4.7-24. This text contains a charge by the adversaries of the community and the answer of the Persian king. Therefore it can be assumed that the term 'Judaean' was not a self-designation, but a designation of the citizen–temple community by its adversaries or the Persian authorities. After 458/457 this term becomes the dominating self-designation, because it sharply distinguished the citizen–temple community from other socio-political structures in Palestine.

The citizen–temple community was in a state of development until 458/457 BCE, and the variety of self-designations conformed to this condition. After 458/457 BCE, when the development of the community was more or less completed, the self-designations became more precise. Therefore, terms which pointed to the domination of the returnees (nos. 1–2) dropped out of use, while other terms (nos. 3–5) were used only with a sharply defined meaning. The term 'Judaean' became the dominant self-designation because it agreed with the separation that the citizen–temple community desired from all the other socio-political structures.

1. J. Pedersen, *Israel: Its Life and Culture*, I-II (Oxford, 1926), pp. 54-57; E.A. Speiser, '*People* and *Nation* in Israel', *JBL* 79 (1960), pp. 157-63.

2. Vogt, *Studien*, pp. 76-89.

III

The development of the citizen–temple community was accomplished in an almost permanent confrontation with the population of Palestine, which stood outside the community. In modern biblical studies, this population is mainly understood as a homogeneous and amorphous entity. But this suggestion is disproved by the data in Ezra–Nehemiah where the adversaries of the community are designated by various terms (Table 2):

	Group	Before 458/457	After 458/457
1.	'Adversaries, enemies'	3	5
2.	'Strange women, strange sons, strangers'	-	10
3.	'Peoples'	-	5
4.	'Peoples of the land'	1	5
5.	'Peoples of the country'	-	4
6.	*'am hā'āreṣ*	1	-

Table 2

Such a varied terminology could be attributed to two factors—a changing subjective attitude of the members of the community towards the 'outside' people or groups, or through the changing constituency and nature of these groups which were outside the community.

From the following summary the term 'peoples of the land' (*'ammê hā'ᵃrāṣôt*, no. 4) can be excluded. It mainly appears in the announcement about divorces of mixed marriages (Ezra 9.1, 2, 11; Neh. 10.29). Since the enumeration of people in Ezra 9.1 agrees with the one in Deut. 7.1-3, one suspects that the designation 'peoples of the land' was a stereotype formula.

Before the rebuilding of the Jerusalem temple started, 'the enemies' (*ṣārîm*) of Judah and Benjamin (Ezra 4.1) submitted a request to Zerubbabel and the heads of the *'ābôt*[1] to allow them to participate in the building. When this offer was rejected, the *'am hā'āreṣ* hindered the hand of Judah's people and inhibited them from building' (Ezra 4.4). In this paragraph, one and the same group of people were called *ṣārîm* (no. 1) and *'am hā'āreṣ* (no. 6).

Since a thorough summary of the literature dedicated to the *'am*

1. J. P. Weinberg, 'Das *Bēit 'Āḇōt* im 6.–4. Jh v.u.Z', *VT* 23 (1973), p. 409.

hā'āreṣ has been undertaken by Amusin,[1] only the recent contribution by Nicholson should be mentioned here. Nicholson emphasizes the indeterminate and various meanings of this term, and stresses that the concrete content and sense must be read from the context and the historical situation.[2]

The interpretations in the existing scientific literature on the character of the postexilic *'am hā'āreṣ* can be summarized as follows: (1) the term *'am hā'āreṣ* describes the members of the postexilic community (Meyer, Nikel, etc.)[3] and (2) the term *'am hā'āreṣ* is a designation of the population in Palestine standing outside the community, mainly the Samarians and the non-deported inhabitants of Judah (Amusin, de Vaux, Kittel, Talmon and Vogt).[4] The existence of such entirely different viewpoints justifies a detailed investigation which should start with an enumeration of the occurrences of the term in the postexilic parts of the Old Testament (Table 3):

586-539/538		539/538–458/457			Second half of 5th c./4th c. and later		
Ezek. 1–39;	Ezek. 40–48	Ezra	Hag.	Zach.	Neh.	Job	Dan.
5	3	1	1	1	-	1	1

Table 3

This table proves that the term *'am hā'āreṣ* appears less in the sixth to fourth centuries BCE than in the first half of the first millennium BCE or in the era of Mishna and Talmud (of about 80 cases in the Old Testament, only 13 refer to the sixth to fourth centuries BCE) and in the majority of these occurences it refers to the time before 458/457 BCE.

As the five references to the term *'am hā'āreṣ* in Ezekiel 1–39 refer to pre-exilic time and society, they prove that in the sixth century BCE the term was used in its pre-exilic meaning as a designation for

1. Amusin, *People*, pp. 14-16.

2. E.W. Nicholson, 'The Meaning of the Expression *'am hā'āres* in the Old Testament', *JSS* 10 (1965), pp. 59-66.

3. E. Meyer, *Die Entstehung des Judentums* (Halle, 1896), pp. 123-28; J. Nikel, *Die Wiederherstellung des jüdischen Gemeinwesens nach dem Exil* (Freiburg, 1900), pp. 66-67.

4. Amusin, *People*, p. 35; R. de Vaux, *Les institutions de l'Ancien Testament*, I (Paris, 1958), pp. 111-13; R. Kittel, *Geschichte des Volkes Israel*, III.2 (Stuttgart, 1929), pp. 433-41; Sh. Talmon, 'The Judean 'Am Hā'āres in Historical Perspective', *PEQ* (1968), p. 87; Vogt, *Studien*, p. 149.

fully-enfranchised citizens. In the texts belonging to the *nāśî*-layer[1] of Ezekiel 45.22; 46.3,9, *'am hā'āreṣ* designates the non-priestly part of the future community.

In Zech. 7.5, the term *'am hā'āreṣ* designates the entire postexilic community. The same appears also in Hag. 2.4: 'And now, Zerubbabel, be comforted, says Yahweh, Jehoshua, son of Jehozadak, be comforted the High priest, the entire *'am hā'āreṣ* be comforted, says Yahweh, and work [meaning build the temple], for I am with you, says Yahweh *Ṣ*ᵉ*bā'ôt*'. The sense of this paragraph is quite clear—the prophet calls upon the *'am hā'āreṣ* to build the temple, and *'am hā'āreṣ* here is the emerging citizen–temple community.

It is clear that *'am hā'āreṣ* was not only a self-designation of the community, but also a designation for its adversaries (Table 2, no. 6). This means that the term describes fundamentally different socio-political structures in Palestine of the sixth to fifth centuries BCE. To overcome this contradiction, Meyer[2] suggested a substitution of *'am hā'āreṣ* in Ezra 4.4 with *'ammê hā'*ᵃ*rāṣôt* (cf. Ezra 3.3). Rothstein[3] identified the *'am hā'āreṣ* in Ezra 4.4 with *hā'ām hazzeh* mentioned in Hag. 2.14, while Amusin[4] suggested that the term *'am hā'āreṣ* in Hag. 2.4 is to be substituted with the expression *š*ᵉ*'ērît hā'ām*, which is often mentioned in Haggai (e.g. 1.12; 2.2).

But there is also another possibility that would overcome this apparent contradiction without any unwarranted emendation of the Masoretic text. It can be assumed that in the sixth to fifth centuries BCE the term *'am hā'āreṣ* contained two fundamentally different meanings and that it was both a self-designation of the emerging citizen–temple community, and a designation for the opposite socio-political structures. This assumption is supported by the fact that the book of Ezra, where *'am hā'āreṣ* is the designation of the enemies of the community, and the books of Haggai and Zechariah, where the community itself is designated with this term, came into being in different circles of the citizen–temple community and belonged to different literary genres. This allows a fundamentally different application of the term

1. H. Gese, *Der Verfassungsentwurf des Ezechiel (Kap. 40–48) traditionsgeschichtlich untersucht* (Tübingen, 1957), pp. 118-22.

2. E. Meyer, *Entstehung*, p. 127.

3. J.W. Rothstein, *Juden und Samaritaner: Die grundlegende Scheidung von Judentum und Heidentum* (Leipzig, 1908), pp. 5-11.

4. Amusin, *People*, pp. 31-32.

in each case. But what is the reason that two opposing socio-political structures were each called *'am hā'āreṣ*?

The use of *'am hā'āreṣ* in Haggai and Zechariah as a self-designation of the community follows an old prophetic tradition and this term is often mentioned in Jeremiah (e.g. 34.19, 52.25), where it designated the fully enfranchised population of Judah. Through the application of this term, the intention is to establish the emerging community as a community of such fully enfranchised members.

The application of the term *'am hā'āreṣ* as a designation for adversaries, mainly the Samarians, can be explained very well through the concrete historical situation in the sixth to fifth centuries BCE. When in 722 BCE the state of Israel was destroyed and about 10% of its population were deported, the Assyrians settled people from different areas of the Assyrian empire in the newly founded province of Samaria (Samerina).[1] Alt's[2] assumption, that the newcomers settled only in Shomron and the surrounding area is refuted by the discoveries of Assyrian and other non-Palestinian pottery in many towns of northern Palestine in the eighth to seventh centuries BCE.[3] It is difficult to agree with Alt's[4] opinion that, in Assyrian Samaria, these newcomers made up the only fully authorized community, which separated totally from the local population and ruled over the latter. The seal from the seventh or sixth centuries BCE from Shechem with the old Hebraic name Mibne or Miqne,[5] or the seal from the eighth or seventh centuries BCE from Megiddo with the inscription '(belonging) to 'Asaph' proves that representatives from the local non-exiled

1. E. Fohrer, *Die Provinzeinteilung des assyrischen Reiches* (Leipzig, 1920), pp. 59-63.

2. A. Alt, 'Das System der assyrischen Provinzen auf dem Boden des Reiches Israel', *KSGVI* 2 (1953), pp. 188-205.

3. G.E. Wright, *Shechem: The Biography of a Biblical City* (New York, 1965), pp. 163-69; J. Gray, 'Tell el Fara' by Nablus: a "Mother" in Ancient Israel', *PEQ* 84 (1952), pp. 110-13; J.P. Free, 'The Seventh Season at Dothan', *BASOR* 160 (1960), pp. 6-15; H.O. Thompson, 'Tell el-Husn–Biblical Beth-shan', *BA* 30 (1967), p. 116; Y. Yadin, 'The Rise and Fall of Hazor', *Archaeology* 10.2 (1957), p. 87; R.S. Lamon and G.M. Shipton, *Megiddo 1: Seasons of 1925–1934* (Chicago, 1939), p. 88.

4. A. Alt, 'Die Rolle Samarias bei der Entstehung des Judentums', *KSGVI 2* (1953), pp. 318-24.

5. Wright, *Shechem*, p. 163; J. Naveh, 'Canaanite and Hebrew Epigraphic Texts' [Hebrew] (1960–1964), *Leš* 30 (1965), pp. 75-76.

population also belonged to the upper class in the Assyrian-Babylonian province of Samaria. The upper class in Samaria was mixed and consisted of representatives of the newcomers, for example Nabuahhe on the ostracon from Shomron (Sukenik, *PQS* [1933], p. 155, no. 1), and the local population. The majority of the inhabitants of Samaria was also mixed, although the non-deported Israelite population predominated.

In this mixed, but by its provenience, predominantly Israelite, population of Samaria, a variation of Yahwism spread, which one may call 'Canaanite Yahwism' (e.g. 2 Kgs 17.25-41).[1] This is the reason why the *ʻam hā'āreṣ* of Ezra 4.2 could say, 'we see your God, just as you do, and we have been offering sacrifices to him from the time of Esarhaddon...' The archaeological finds in Palestine point to a sharp contrast between the Judah of the sixth century BCE, which was in ruins, and the bustling northern and western provinces in Palestine. It is not by chance that the majority of the imported pottery was found in the north and west of Palestine (Tell Abu Hawam, Atlit, Ashkelon, Tell Jemme, for example).[2] It also has to be noted that Samaria was a province of the Persian empire, whose governors were mainly representatives from the local population (Ezra 4.8-10).

In comparison with the emerging citizen–temple community, the Samarians were better established in many respects economically and administratively. Therefore it seems to be obvious to designate this community of free and mainly fully enfranchised people with the term *ʻam hā'āreṣ* which is usual for such a community. The application of the term for the emerging community and the Samarians was even more justified around 520 BCE, since at that time the tendency toward separation of the citizen–temple community did not yet exist. But it has to be emphasized that the designation *ʻam hā'āreṣ*, when applied to a community in opposition to the postexilic community, gave rise to a further semantic evolution of the term.

After 458/457 BCE, the term *ʻam hā'āreṣ* as a self-designation for the community or as a designation for adversaries is not used any more. For the latter, other terms (Table 2, nos. 2–3) are used, because at this time the inner structure and the position of the citizen–temple

1. E. Janssen, *Juda in der Exilszeit: Ein Beitrag zur Frage der Entstehung des Judentums* (FRLANT, 51/69; Göttingen, 1956), pp. 57-68.

2. D. Auscher, 'Les relations entre la Grèce et la Palestine avant la conquête d'Alexandre', *VT* 17 (1967), pp. 9-21.

community underwent significant changes. There were increasing numbers of members of the community, an expansion of its territory,[1] an economic consolidation of the *bāttê 'ābôt* and important structural changes within the community as well as the privileges granted by Artaxerxes I—all of which furthered the formation of the citizen–temple community as a self-reliant socio-political organism.[2] All these new aspects fundamentally changed the position of the community in Palestine, and also affected the other socio-political formations in the country, although the citizen–temple community remained administratively subordinate to the Samarian province from the end of the sixth century until the first half of the fifth century BCE. Because of the expansion of the community territory in the southern and south-western direction,[3] more and more members of the citizen–temple community also appeared within the provinces of Idumea, Ashdod and others.[4] In these provinces, the attitudes of the community members to the socio-political authorities, on whose ground they lived, were indifferent or even hostile because they felt connected only with the citizen–temple community (Neh. 4.6; 5.7). Therefore it is conceivable that the opposition to the citizen–temple community not only became stronger but also included other socio-political formations in Palestine after 458/457 BCE. As the citizen–temple community changed, the composition of its adversaries changed and correspondingly new terms were used to designate these adversaries.

In the report about the break up of mixed marriages (Ezra 10; Neh. 13) the following terms are applied: 'strange women, strange sons, strangers' (Table 2, no. 2; Ezra 10.2, 11; Neh. 9.2; 13.27, 30) and 'peoples of the land' (no. 5, *'ammê hā'āreṣ*, Ezra 10.2, 11; Neh. 10.31, 32). In the Old Testament the word *nēkār* designates something absolutely strange and non-Yahwistic (Deut. 9.21; 1 Kgs 8.41). 'Strange women from the peoples of the land' (Ezra 10.2) were women from Ashdod, Ammon and Moab

1. Weinberg, 'Demographische Notizen', pp. 56-57.

2. J.P. Weinberg, 'Zentral- und Partikulargewalt in achämenidischen Reich', *Klio* 59 (1977), pp. 25-42.

3. Weinberg, 'Demographische Notizen', pp. 56-57.

4. B. Maisler (Mazar), *Excavations in Tell Qasileh* [Hebrew], *E-I* 1 (1951), pp. 68-69, Tab. XI.6; M. Dothan, 'Ashdod of the Philistines', in D.N. Freedman and J.C. Greenfield (eds.), *New Directions in Biblical Archaeology* (New York, 1971), p. 25.

(Neh. 10.31; 13.23). *'ammê hā'āreṣ* is not simply the plural form from *'am hā'āreṣ* and between the two terms there is an essential difference; *'am hā'āreṣ* is always a designation for a Yahwistic community, while *'ammê hā'āreṣ* designates totally strange and non-Yahwistic communities. There is a good reason for the members of the citizen–temple community to conceive of the *'ammê hā'āreṣ* as *nēkār*, that is, something totally strange. The archaeological finds from Ashdod[1] not only prove that the culture of the Phoenicians living there was differently composed, but also that the level of economic development and wealth was higher in comparison with Judah.[2]

Often the adversaries of the citizen–temple community are also designated as 'peoples' (Table 2, no. 3, *gôyim*, Neh. 5.8, 9; 6.16). Speiser[3] proved that in the Old Testament the term *gôy* signifies the connection between a people and the state, that is, a politically organized people. The designation *gôyim* for these adversaries was legal because the people who fought against the citizen–temple community in the second half of the fifth century BCE (e.g. Neh. 2–6) had a certain statehood in the form of provinces. Sanballat (e.g. Neh. 2.19; 3.34) was *paḥat šamrayin* (Cowley 30.29)[4], which means governor of this Persian province, and 'Tobiya, the Ammonite servant' (e.g. Neh. 2.10), was probably the governor of the province Ammon.[5] The third participant in this coalition, 'the Arab Geshem' (Neh. 2.19; 6.1), was a nebulous figure until quite recently. But the inscription on a silver vessel from the fifth century BCE from Tell el-Maskhuta (Egypt) 'Kainu, son of Geshem, King of Kedar', allows one to assume that Geshem was an influential and powerful vassal of the Persian kings in the south of Palestine,[6] and therefore also a leader of a *gôy*.

1. M. Dothan and D.N. Freedman, 'Ashdod 1', *Atiqot* 7 (1967), pp. 5-13; M. Dothan, 'Ashdod: A City of the Philistine Pentapolis', *Archaeology* 20.3 (1967), p. 186.

2. E. Stern, 'The Land of Israel during the Persian Period' [Hebrew], *Qadmoniyot* 2.4 (1969), pp. 114-23.

3. Speiser, *People*, pp. 157-63.

4. A.E. Cowley, *Aramaic Papyri of the Fifth Century BC* (Oxford, 1954).

5. B. Mazar, 'The Tobiads', *IEJ* 7 (1957), pp. 3-4.

6. I. Rabinowitz, 'Aramaic Inscriptions of the Fifth Century BCE from a North-Arab Shrine in Egypt', *JNES* 15 (1956), pp. 1-9.

IV

Our investigations allow for several conclusions:

1. The self-designation of the citizen–temple community changed according to the development of the community in the sixth to fourth centuries BCE. With the development of the community after 458/457 BCE into a self-reliant and unique socio-political organism the term *'am hā'āreṣ*, taken from the first half of the first millennium BCE, disappeared because the community preferred self-designations which more precisely expressed its character.

2. In the sixth to fourth centuries BCE the citizen–temple community encountered different socio-political formations. Each of them had unique features and its own attitude to the citizen–temple community, whose members used different terms—*'am hā'āreṣ*, *'ammê hā'āreṣ*, *gôyim*, etc.—to designate their adversaries. Each of these terms corresponded more or less with the socio-political adversaries of the community and expressed the communities' attitude to these different formations.

3. In the sixth to fifth centuries BCE, the term *'am hā'āreṣ* designated adversaries of the developing citizen–temple community, mainly the Samarians, and was also used as a self-designation of the community and its non-priestly part. After 458/457 BCE the role and influence of the priesthood in the community became noticeably stronger. Jerusalem as the seat of the high priest became more and more important and the entire citizen–temple community gradually became the leading power in Palestine. At the same time, the influence and the importance of the laymen in the community, and the Samarians outside the community designated as *'am hā'āreṣ*, decreased. The term *'am hā'āreṣ* took on a degrading sense and through an intensification of the class conflict within Hellenistic-Roman Palestine, the degradation implied by the term *'am hā'āres* became stronger, as a popular saying points out: "When I still was a man from the *'am hā'āreṣ*, I would say: 'Whoever gives me a scribe, I will bite him like a donkey" ' (*b. Pes*. 49b).

Chapter 5

N^e^tînîm AND 'SONS OF THE SLAVES OF SOLOMON' IN THE SIXTH TO FOURTH CENTURIES BCE

I

A general consensus in modern biblical studies is unfortunately a rare occurrence. This makes the general consensus with regard to the origin and nature of the *n^e tînîm* and the 'sons of the slaves of Solomon' all the more surprising. Yet in this case there is no evidence for a final solution of the problem, only a rather long-standing attachment to a hypothesis that has been proposed for over a century.

The viewpoint of J. Wellhausen[1] that the *n^e tînîm* were drawn from the 'heathen' temple servants, that is *hierodouloi*, was taken up by W. Baudissin[2] who suggested that the origin of the *n^e tînîm* was from the Gibeonites (Josh. 9.27). Baudissin also expressed the opinion that in the Achaemenid period, the *n^e tînîm* had the status of a *gēr*—that is foreign people who were free, but not fully enfranchised. According to A. Bertholet,[3] the postexilic *n^e tînîm* were descendants of prisoners of war who were given to the first temple in Jerusalem as temple slaves.

Similar ideas about the *n^e tînîm* are repeated, although not without various modifications, in the studies of Meyer, Kittel, Braude, Häusler, de Vaux, Mowinckel, Kreissig and others.[4] For example, in

1. J. Wellhausen, *Prolegomena zur Geschichte Israels* (1899), p. 145.

2. W. Baudissin, *Die Geschichte des alttestamentlichen Priestertums* (1889), pp. 29-32, 98-100, 142-51.

3. A. Bertholet, *Die Stellung der Israeliten und der Juden zu den Fremden* (Leipzig, 1896), pp. 51-52.

4. E. Meyer, *Die Entstehung des Judentums* (1896), pp. 180-82; R. Kittel, *Geschichte des Volkes Israel*, III (1929), pp. 417-19; W.G. Braude, *Jewish Proselytes in the First Five Centuries of the Common Era* (1940), pp. 33, 37; E. Häusler, *Sklaven und Personen minderen Rechts im Alten Testament* (1956),

Meyer's view, a late 'leviticalization' of the *n*^e^*tînîm*, along with the 'sons of the slaves of Solomon' is presumed, while according to Braude, this assumption is false.

The view that the *n*^e^*tînîm* were slaves or servants of the first temple, and also belonged to the temple personnel in the sixth to fourth centuries BCE, was supported indirectly through the study of Daugherty,[1] who made reference to the typological proximity of the Old Testament *n*^e^*tînîm* to the Babylonian temple slaves,[2] the *širkutu*.[3] According to Mendelsohn,[4] the first Jerusalem temple had its specific slaves—*n*^e^*tînîm*—who formed 'a hereditary caste of temple slaves...', while the designation 'sons of the slaves of Solomon' was a *terminus technicus* for the pre-exilic Palestinian state slaves which are otherwise widely attested in the ancient Orient. In the sixth to fourth centuries BCE these latter were joined to the *n*^e^*tînîm*. While agreeing with the relationship between Gibeonites and *n*^e^*tînîm*, Haran[5] further emphasized that the latter were 'a conglomeration of ethnically heterogeneous slaves...', which belonged to the temple, and who 'had no juridical or practical possibility of shaking off their slavery.'

The view of Hölscher,[6] that the assignment of the *n*^e^*tînîm* to the temple personnel could not be proven, was already a departure from the generally-held perspective. Levine[7] stressed that the Old Testament tradition never associates the *n*^e^*tînîm* with the Gibeonites, and *n*^e^*tînîm* are nowhere seen as temple slaves. Accordingly, his view

pp. 121-23; R. de Vaux, *Les institutions de l'Ancien Testament*, I (1958), p. 138; S. Mowinckel, *Studien zu dem Buche Ezra–Nehemia*, I (1964), p. 79; H. Kreissig, *Die sozialökonomische Situation in Juda zur Achämenidenzeit* (1973), pp. 75-76.

1. R.P. Daugherty, *The Shirkutu of Babylonia Deities* (London, 1923), pp. 90-91.

2. M.A. Dandamaev ('Temple Farmers in Late Babylonia' [Russian], *PS* 17 [1967], pp. 41-49) points out that on estates of the Babylonian temples slaves (*širku*) worked as well as dependent peasants (*ikkaru*).

3. A similar view is expressed by A.G. Perichanian, *The Temple Communities of Asia Minor and Armenia* [Russian] (Moscow, 1959), pp. 113-16.

4. I. Mendelsohn, *Slavery in the Ancient Near East* (New York, 1949), pp. 100-106.

5. M. Haran, 'The Gibeonites, the Nethinim and the Sons of Solomon's Servants', *VT* 11 (1961), pp. 159-69.

6. G. Hölscher, 'Levi', *RE*, XII (1925), p. 2185.

7. B.A. Levine, 'The Netinim', *JBL* 82 (1963), pp. 207-12.

was that the *n^e tînîm* were 'members of a cultic guild' and the 'sons of the slaves of Solomon' were 'members of a guild of royal merchants'. According to Shiffman,[1] the *n^e tînîm* provided services to the Levites, while the 'sons of the slaves of Solomon' were descendants of Solomon's freedmen.

Apart from the specific disagreements, modern biblical scholarship proposes that the *n^e tînîm* and the 'sons of the slaves of Solomon' are the descendants of the servants or slaves of the first Jerusalem temple, and also belonged to the temple personnel in the sixth to fourth centuries BCE.

II

Sources for information about the *n^e tînîm* and the 'sons of the slaves of Solomon' are found in the Talmud, in the works of Josephus, in 1 Esdras and pre-eminently in the postexilic portions of the Old Testament. It is worthwhile to review the available data in reversed chronological order.

One reads in *m. Qiddušin* 4.1 that 'ten hereditary castes came up out of Babylon—priests, Levites, Israelites, ones who were dedicated, proselytes, freedmen, *n^e tînîm*, enslaved and foundlings'. In *m. Hurayoth* 3.8, however, this rank-ordering is made more precise: 'a priest goes before a Levite, a Levite before an Israelite, an Israelite before the child of a whore; the child of a whore before a *nātîn*, a *nātîn* before a proselyte, a proselyte before a freed slave'. This, and other (*m. Yebamoth* 2.4; 6.1) remarks allow little doubt that the Talmudic tradition assigns the *n^e tînîm* to the lowest levels of the social pyramid. They are not seen as fully-fledged members of the community and a judgment is not legal if the judge is 'a proselyte, a child of a whore, a *netin* or an old man' (*m. Horayoth* 1.4). In order to provide the basis for such a negative view of the *n^e tînîm*, R. Hana b. Ada taught that the *n^e tînîm* descended from the Gibeonites and other Canaanite *gērîm* (*b. Yebamoth* 78b-79b).

The perspective of the Talmudic tradition with regard to the *n^e tînîm* is clearly negative. These people do not belong to the temple personnel and they are certainly not fully-enfranchised members of

1. I.S. Shiffman, 'The Legal Status of Slaves in Judah according to Old Testament Tradition' [Russian], *VDI* 3 (1964), p. 57.

the community, and stand on the lowest level of the social pyramid.[1] It must be said, however, that the actual existence of the *n^e^tînîm* in the Talmudic era is debatable, and the relevant legislation is quite possibly only theoretically meaningful.[2]

In the eleventh chapter of the *Antiquitates Judaicae*, the *n^e^tînîm* and the 'sons of the slaves of Solomon' are generally not mentioned, although Josephus repeatedly enumerated different categories of the temple personnel. Certainly in the cases where Josephus agrees with the Masoretic Text, he (and the translator of 1 Esdras) substitutes the concept *n^e^tînîm* with *hierodouloi* (temple servants), for example in *Ant*. 11.3.10 (in comparison with 1 Esdras and the MT).

	Ant. 11.3.10	1 Esd. 5. 29-35	Neh. 7.43-60	= Ezra 2.40-58
Levites	74	74	74	74
Singers	128	128	148	128
Gatekeepers	110	139	138	139
Hierodouloi	392	372	392	392

A comparison of these parallel texts reveals that already the translator of 1 Esdras departed from the Masoretic model by his transformation of the *n^e^tînîm* from the MT to 'temple servants' (*hierodouloi*), but the 'sons of the slaves of Solomon' remained as is. The rendering of the word *n^e^tînîm* with the Greek (*hierodouloi*) is not a technique that is common to the translator of the Septuagint, for in other places in the LXX (2 Esd. 2.43-58; 17.46, 60) *n^e^tînîm* is not translated, but merely transcribed. Josephus[3] adopted the word *hierodouloi*, but left out the term 'sons of the slaves of Solomon' even though he knew the exact wording of the Masoretic text, which is obvious when one considers the precise agreement of the total number (392) of the *n^e^tînîm* and the 'sons of the slaves of Solomon' in Neh. 7.60 = Ezra 2.58 with the *hierodouloi* in *Ant*. 11.3.10.

1. J.M. Baumgarten ('The Exclusion of Netinim and Proselytes in 4 Q Florilegium', *RQ* 29 [1972], pp. 87-96) is of the opinion that in the Talmudic tradition the *n^e^tînîm* were held to be in the same category as illegitimates. His conclusion about the negative attitude of the Qumranites is acceptable, although the reference to 4 Q Florilegium 2.4-6 does not entirely convince.

2. H. Kreissig, *Die sozialen Zusammenhänge des judäischen Krieges* (1970), p. 78.

3. On the relationship between 1 Esdras and the corresponding parts in *Ant*., cf. S. Mowinckel, *Studien zu dem Buche Ezra–Nehemia*, I (Oslo, 1964), pp. 19-28.

But this raises the question of whether this omission of *n*^{e}*tînîm* is an expression of a personal opinion or a reflection of the actual circumstances of the temple personnel in the relevant era.[1] The sources of this time refer neither to *n*^{e}*tînîm* nor 'sons of the slaves of Solomon' in the role of temple personnel, but occasionally one reads that Levites who are active as singers, scribes and supervisors in the temple are called *hierodouloi*. In any case, after 200 BCE,[2] the *n*^{e}*tînîm* (and the 'sons of the slaves of Solomon') do not belong to the temple personnel and are not seen in that capacity.

III

For our discussion, it is useful to look at the etymology and semantics of the relevant terminology.

The word *nātîn* is a derivative of the verbal root *ntn* (to give, given; more seldom, dedicated)[3] and thus in its participial form would be 'one given' without involving sacred obligations. Gray and Levine[4] refer to the Ugaritic term *ytnm*, which in their opinion designates a particular category of temple servants. But the text C115 (UT 301), in which this word is found, is a receipt of taxes-in-kind (wine) to the treasury, and the word *spr ytnm* should be translated as 'register of paying (taxes)', and thus has nothing to do with temple servants.

In the term 'sons of the slaves of Solomon', the name is without doubt that of the well-known king. The word *bēn* (son) can, besides its simple meaning, also indicate the membership of an individual to an ethnic, kinship or professional community,[5] and is frequently this way in Ezra–Nehemiah.[6] Thus, in the term 'sons of the slaves of Solomon', the term *ben* indicates membership of a socio-professional group, which is called 'slaves of Solomon'. The word *'ebed* means 'slave' in the direct sense, although in the Old Testament (2 Sam. 14.19-20;

1. A. Büchler, *Die Priester und der Cultus im letzten Jahrzehnt des jerusalemischen Tempels* (1895), pp. 119-35; H. Kreissig, *Die sozialen Zusammenhänge*, p. 78.
2. *Terminus post quem* for 1 Esdras (A. Bentzen, *Introduction to the Old Testament*, II [Copenhagen, 1957], pp. 219-20).
3. E.A. Speiser, 'Unrecognized Dedication', *IEJ* 13 (1963), pp. 69-73.
4. J. Gray, *Archaeology and the Old Testament* (1962), p. 116; B.A. Levine, *The Netinim*, p. 208.
5. G. Brin, 'On the Title, *Son of the King*', *Leš* 31 (1966), pp. 5-20.
6. J.P. Weinberg, 'Das *Bēit 'Ābōt* im 6.–4. Jh. v.u.Z.', *VT* 23 (1973), p. 408.

2 Kgs 22.12) and in epigraphic material it is often used as an indication of someone of high rank.[1]

The etymology and semantics of both relevant terms do not necessarily indicate a religious meaning, nor an absolute association of the groups thus named with the cult or temple.

IV

Most of the evidence about *n^{e}tînîm* and 'sons of the slaves of Solomon' are found in Ezra–Nehemiah. For a fuller explanation, the authentic list in Neh. 7.7-69 = Ezra 2.2-67 is of particular importance. As I have previously argued,[2] this list whose original *Sitz im Leben* is to be found in Nehemiah 7, is a register of the collectives of the citizen–temple community until the year 458/7 (Table 1).

	Designation	Collective	Men[3]	Percentages
1	'Men of the people of Israel'	17	16,722/15,520*	54.9/53.2
2	Collectives named after localities	14/16	8684/8635	28.5/29.6
3	Priests	4	4289	14.2/14.7
4	Levites	1	74	0.2
5	Singers	1	148/128	0.5/0.4
6	Gatekeepers	6	138/139	0.4/0.5
7	*N^{e}tînîm* and 'sons of the slaves of Solomon'	42/45	392	1.3/1.4

* The first number is from Nehemiah 7, the second from Ezra 2.

Table 1

From the data in this table, much of which is important to our investigation, it can perhaps be assumed that the *n^{e}tînîm* and 'sons of the slaves of Solomon' are on the lowest level of the socio-professional pyramid of the postexilic community (compare the assignment of the *n^{e}tînîm* by the Talmud); although according to the data the number of the collectives and persons, indicate that a higher place in the ranking is possible.

For our continued analysis it is worthwhile to enumerate all the 32/35 collectives of the *n^{e}tînîm* and the ten collectives of 'sons of the

1. Shiffman, *Legal Status* [Russian], pp. 55-56.

2. J.P. Weinberg, 'Demographische Notizen zur Geschichte der nachexilischen Gemeinde in Juda', *Klio* 54 (1972), pp. 51-53.

3. G.E. Mendenhall, 'The Census List of Numbers 1 and 26', *JBL* 77 (1958), pp. 52-66; Weinberg, 'Demographische Notizen', p. 52.

slaves of Solomon' that are mentioned in Neh. 7.46-59 = Ezra 2.43-58:

N^e^tînîm

	Designation		Designation		Designation
1	Ziha	13	Reaiah	25	Bazlith/Bazluth*
2	Hasupha	14	Rezin	26	Mehida
3	Tabbaoth	15	Nekoda	27	Harsha
4	Keros*	16	Gazzam	28	Barkos
5	Sia/Siaha*	17	Uzza	29	Sisera
6	Padon	18	Paseah	30	Temah
7	Lebana	19	Besai	31	Neziah
8	Hagaba	20	Meumim	32	Hatipha
9	Shalmai/Shamlai*	21	Nephushesim/Nephisim	33	Akkub**
10	Hanan	22	Bakbuk	34	Hagab***
11	Giddel	23	Hakupha	35	Asnav
12	Gahar	24	Harhur	36	Gishpa****

* The first name for Nehemiah 7, the second for Ezra 2.
** Nos. 33-35 are only mentioned in Ezra 2.
*** No. 34 in Ezra 2 is the repetition of no. 8 in Nehemiah 7 = Ezra 2.
**** No. 36 is only mentioned in Nehemiah 11.21 and possibly identical to no. 2 in Nehemiah 7 = Ezra 2.

'Sons of the slaves of Solomon'.

	Designation		Designation
1	Sotai	6	Giddel
2	Sophereth/Hassophereth	7	Shepatiah
3	Perida/Peruda	8	Hattil
4	Jaala/Jaalah	9	Pochereth-hazzebaim
5	Darkon	10	Amon/'Ami

Table 2

An onomastic investigation of the names of the 32 and 35 collectives listed in Table 2 reveals that 15 (c. 45%) names do not otherwise occur in old Hebrew onomastics. The percentage of such unique names is much higher amongst the *n^e^tînîm* than in the names of the other socio-professional groups of the postexilic community, which indicates the existence of a unique tradition of names already familiar in the sixth to fifth centuries BCE among the *n^e^tînîm*.

An onomastic analysis of the remaining 17 and 18 names, that is, the names not unique and thus comparable with the onomastic material that is available in old Hebrew, gives rise to three questions: (1) Do the relevant collectives of the *n^e^tînîm* have a pre-exilic root or not?

(2) In which milieu[1] of the pre-exilic era does one locate the names from collectives whose names do have pre-exilic roots? (3) In which area of pre-exilic Palestine can these collectives of *n*^{e}*tînîm* be located?

1	Pre-exilic	Postexilic	Unknown
	58%	-	42%
2	Priestly	Non-Priestly	Unknown
	0/10%	48/38%	52%
3	Judah	Palestine	Unknown
	52/42%	0/10%	48%

Table 3

Part one of this table shows that the majority of collectives of *n*^{e}*tînîm* had pre-exilic roots. This conclusion can be also strengthened through epigraphic material. An ostracon from Arad (beginning of sixth century BCE) contains the name Qerosi [2] (cf. no. 4 in Table 2). Part three shows that the majority of the names of the *n*^{e}*tînîm* (nos. 4, 7, 8, 9, 13, 18, 20, 21, 22 and 23) are to be located in pre-exilic Judah. Similarly, the presence of names constructed from designations of animals and plants attests to this, since this is a recognizable characteristic of names from southern Judah.[3] An investigation of the onomastica of the postexilic priests and Levites shows that some 60% of its collectives are rooted in the pre-exilic priesthood. But among the *n*^{e}*tînîm*, as part two indicates, the similarity with the pre-exilic priesthood is not particularly striking. Similarly, one notes the circumstance that 90% of the names of the postexilic priests contain theophoric elements, 82% among the Levites, while amongst the names of the *n*^{e}*tînîm*, there is only about 20%. Such a small percentage of theophorous nomenclature among the *n*^{e}*tînîm* is hardly believable if they belong to temple personnel.

If, for the time being, one sets aside the unique names among the onomastica of the 'sons of the slaves of Solomon', then there remain only six noteworthy names suitable for an onomastic analysis. The results of this analysis are summarized thus:

1. The term 'milieu' signifies the social/ professional circle in which the roots of the collective are to be located.

2. Y. Aharoni, 'Hebrew Ostraca from Tel Arad', *IEJ* 16 (1966), pp. 5-6.

3. G.B. Gray, *Studies in Hebrew Proper Names* (1896), pp. 86-115; M. Noth, *Die israelitischen Personennamen im Rahmen der gemeinsemitischen Namengebung* (1928), pp. 229-30.

1	Pre-exilic	Postexilic	Unknown
	83%	-	17%
2	Priestly	Non-Priestly	Unknown
	-	83%	17%
3	Judah	Palestine	Unknown
	67%	-	23%

Table 4

Table 4 illustrates that the majority of collectives of the 'sons of the slaves of Solomon' are rooted in pre-exilic, Jewish, but not priestly, contexts, and this is notably confirmed by the fact that only two names, (nos. 6 and 7) are theophoric in the onomastica of these collectives.

On this point many scholars[1] have concluded that there is a striking number of foreign, non-Hebrew names among the *n^e^tînîm* and the 'sons of the slaves of Solomon'. Such names compose some 68% of the onomastica of *n^e^tînîm* and some 33–40% of the onomastica of 'sons of the slaves of Solomon', which is a much higher percentage when compared with the average of non-Hebrew foreign names among the other socio-professional groups of the postexilic community.

V

In this connection the recent epigraphic data must be taken into consideration, particularly an ostracon found in Arad. This ostracon, which was discovered amongst many others in an area inside the city wall of stratum VI, can be dated to 598 or 586.[2] As Aharoni's previous reading and translation raise no major objections, I cite here the published form of the relevant ostracon:

1	*'l 'dny 'ly*	1	To my Lord Elia-
2	*šb yhwh yš*	2	shib. Yahwe may as-
3	*'l lšlm w't*	3	k for thy peace. And now
4	*tn lšmryhw*	4	give Shemariahu
5	*(?) wlqrsy*	5	. . . and to Qerosi

1. Bertholet, *Die Stellung*, pp. 51-52; Daugherty, *The Shirkutu*, p. 91; Haran, *The Gibeonites*, pp. 166-67.

2. Y. Aharoni, *Hebrew Ostraca*, p. 1; in his later work, 'The Seals of Royal Officers from Arad' [Hebrew], *E-I* 8 (1967), p. 103, Y. Aharoni spoke for a dating of the destruction of Stratum VI in the year 598/597.

6	*ttn (?) wld*	6	give. . . and regarding the
7	*br 'šr ṣ*	7	matter which thou com-
8	*wtny šlm*	8	mandest me— *Shalom*
9	*byt yhwh*	9	in the house of Yahweh
10	*h' yšb*	10	he dwells

Aharoni[1] identified the Eliashib of this ostracon with the owner of three stamps—Eliashib, son of Eshiyahu. On the basis of the fact that this stamp is assigned to the Stratum VII, whose destruction is located at c. 640–625, Aharoni[2] argued that Eliashib, son of Eshiyahu, served in Arad more than 30 years and administrated the supply and distribution of food in Arad. He delivered bread to the *kittiyim* (Greek mercenaries)[3] as well as wine and oil. Aharoni is of the opinion that Eliashib was a *nāgîd 'al hā' ôṣārôt* (1 Chron. 26.24) in Arad, and administered 'all the affairs of God and king' there (v. 32).

In the ostracon from Arad, as is also the case with the letters from Lachish, the sender is customarily not mentioned, probably because the reader knows exactly from where, and from which official or officer, the order came. Nevertheless, in one ostracon from Arad, the sender is mentioned: 'Hananiahu wishes Eliashib peace and welfare to your house. . . '[4] The name Hananiahu, the proper name or father's name of the sender, was among the Benjaminite aristocracy in the pre-exilic era (e.g. 1 Chron. 8.23, 24, 38; 9.44) and well placed in priestly-prophetic circles associated with Jerusalem and the king's palace (e.g. 2 Chron. 16.7; 19.2; 20.34; Jer. 28.1).

In line 10, a 'house of Yahweh' is mentioned, referring either to a temple of the tenth to eighth centuries BCE in Arad, or to the Jerusalem temple. Noting that the temple in Arad was destroyed c. 734 BCE, and there is no information given about its reconstruction,[5] it follows that the temple of Jerusalem is the one referred to.[6] The crux of our investigation is in lines 86-110, and especially the word

1. Aharoni, *Seals*, p. 103.
2. Aharoni, *Seals*, p. 103.
3. Aharoni, *Hebrew Ostraca*, pp. 4-5.
4. Y. Aharoni, *Qadmoniyot* 1 (1968), p. 102.
5. Y. Aharoni and R. Amiran, 'Arad, a Biblical City in Southern Palestine', *Archaeology* 17 (1964), pp. 43-53.
6. Y. Aharoni, 'Hebrew Epigraphy from Tel Arad' [Hebrew], *Yediot* 30 (1966), pp. 36-38.

šlm. These lines have been variously translated as follows:

Y. Aharoni[1]: 'Shalom he dwells in the house of Yahweh'
B.A. Levine[2]: 'he will remit the *šelem*-offer of the temple of Yahwe. . . '
D.N. Freedman[3]: 'it has been settled. In the house of Yahweh he remains. . . '

The construction of the sentence with the verbal root *yšb* (to be situated, remain, live, dwell) makes it likely that here *šlm* is the proper name *Shlomo* or *Shallum*, that was associated with a very ancient Jerusalemite tradition,[4] and was widely distributed in the onomastica of the Jewish priesthood and nobility. Yet another detail must be noted. The majority of the ostraca addressed to Eliashib begin with a short appeal: 'To Eliashib and now'. In the relevant ostracon we find a full and familiar opening formula (lines 1-2) which is also present in the confidential letters from Lachish (e.g. I Lach. II, 1-2; IV, 1; V.1-2) and from Arad.[5] It is particularly important and informative for us that the letter of Hananiahu (or the son of Hananiahu) to Eliashib begins with this familiar opening formula.

Now we can attempt to reconstruct the content of the correspondence that is reflected in the relevant ostraca. Eliashib, a highly-placed royal functionary in Arad, is interested in the fate of one named Shallum or Shelomo; Hananiahu (or the son of Hananiahu) reports in a confidential message, the Shallum or Shelomo is in the Jerusalem temple, and Eliashib is engaged to pass something on to Shemariahu and Qerosi. One can assume, the Shemariahu and Qerosi were officials of the Jerusalem correspondent. Aharoni[6] (with reference to Mazar) suggests that Qerosi was a member of the similarly-named family of *neṯînîm* (cf. no. 4 of the *neṯînîm* in Table 2).

1. Aharoni, *Hebrew Ostraca*, pp. 5-6.
2. B.A. Levine, 'Notes on a Hebrew Ostracon from Arad', *IEJ* 19 (1969), pp. 49-51.
3. D.N. Freedman, 'The Orthography of the Arad Ostraca', *IEJ* 19 (1969), p. 56.
4. N.W. Porteous, 'Jerusalem–Zion: The Growth of a Symbol', in *Verbannung und Heimkehr: Beiträge zur Geschichte und Theologie Israels im 6 und 5 Jahrhundert v. Chr.* (Tübingen, 1961), pp. 239-40.
5. Y. Aharoni, *The Ostraca*, p. 102; 'Three Hebrew Ostraca from Arad', *BASOR* 197 (1970), pp. 28-32.
6. Aharoni, *Hebrew Ostraca*, pp. 5-6; compare Levine, notes pp. 49- 51.

If these suggestions are not mistaken, the ostracon from Arad permits the assumption, that at the beginning of the sixth century BCE, a member of the *n*ᵉ*tînîm*-family Qeros was in the service of the Jewish royal administration.

VI

If we turn once again to an inventory of the members of the citizen–temple community (Table 1), we find no evidence there of the association of the *n*ᵉ*tînîm* and the 'sons of the slaves of Solomon' with the temple personnel in the sixth to fifth centuries BCE. Quite to the contrary, in the information about the residential palace of the community members, we read: 'And the priests, and the Levites and the gatekeepers and the singers, and from the people and the *n*ᵉ*tînîm* and all Israel dwelled in their cities...' (Neh. 7.73).

In this sentence, it is surprising that the 'sons of the slaves of Solomon' are not mentioned, although all remaining socio-professional groups from Neh. 7 = Ezra 2 are counted. It is to be observed that in Neh. 7.60 = Ezra 2.58, after a separate total of the collective of the *n*ᵉ*tînîm* and the collective of the 'sons of the slaves of Solomon', the total number of members in both groups is mentioned. In the list found in Neh. 7 = Ezra 2, it is an exception because the total number of the members of other socio-professional groups always comes after the enumeration of all the collectives belonging to those groups. This special case in Neh. 7.60 = Ezra 2.58, as well as the omission of the 'sons of the slaves of Solomon' in Neh. 7.73, proves that already before 458/7 BCE a coalescing of both these groups had begun.

One can also recognize the fact that in Neh. 7.72, on the first level, the four categories of the priesthood are mentioned (priests, Levites, gatekeepers, singers), then the 'people', then the *n*ᵉ*tînîm*. Keeping in mind that the hierarchy of socio-professional groups is always strictly observed, the striking differentiation of the *n*ᵉ*tînîm* from the priesthood,[1] and its proximity to the lay people can hardly be an accident. In Neh. 10.40 and 13.5, where all categories of the postexilic priesthood are enumerated, the *n*ᵉ*tînîm* are absent, allowing one to assume that also in the sixth to fifth centuries BCE, the *n*ᵉ*tînîm* and the 'sons of the slaves of Solomon' did not belong to the temple personnel.

1. H.C.M. Vogt, *Studie zur nachexilischen Gemeinde in Esra–Nehemia* (1966), pp. 76-84.

How can this assumption be reconciled with the mention of *n^e^tînîm* in the authentic edict of Artaxerxes I from the year 458/7 (Ezra 7.24)? The edict released different groups of the citizen–temple community from taxation and tribute by order of the Persian king (v. 24). In Table 5, the groups mentioned in the edict are compared with those counted in the inventory in Neh. 7 = Ezra 2 in Table 1:

	Nehemiah 7 = Ezra 2		Ezra 7.24
1	Men of the people Israel		-
2	collectives named after localities		-
3	Priests	1	Priests
4	Levites	2	Levites
5	Singers	3	Singers
6	Gatekeepers	4	Gatekeepers
7	*N^e^tînîm* and sons of the slaves of Solomon	5	*N^e^tînîm*
		6	'*pal^e^ḥîn* of the House of God'

Table 5

In this table, two dates capture our attention. First, in the edict of Artaxerxes I, the non-priestly groups of the postexilic community (nos. 1-2 in column 1) are not mentioned; secondly, in the edict there appears a new group, namely '*pal^e^ḥîn* of the House of God'.

The word *pālaḥ* is the participle form of the Aramaic verbal root *plḥ* (work, serve). In the Old Testament, this word and its derivatives occur 11 times; Ezra 7.19, and 24, and then nine times in Daniel (e.g. 3.12, 14; 6.17) where the verb is associated with the word 'God' or to a pronoun for 'God', that is to say, with pronounced religious meaning. The verb *plḥ* and its derivatives are also known in Aramaic epigraphy, where it is often used without religious connotations. In a manumission from Elephantine (427 BCE) a freed slave and his child commit themselves 'to serve' their owner further; in the story of *Aḥiqar* one reads, 'I am old, I cannot work in the gate of the palace and do my service to you' (*lmplḥ*) (Cowley, *Aḥiq*. II, 17); in *CIS* II, 3944,4 the relevant term indicates a soldier. The supposition that the verb *plḥ* and its derivatives are without religious association in non-biblical linguistic use can be supported on wider grounds—as Diakanoff has pointed out to me, the Aramaic *plḥ* is to be associated with the Akkadian (Assyrian dialect) *plh* (work), with the Syriac *gabrê pallāhâ* (men, peasants), as also with the Arabic *flḥ* (work) and *fallāḥ* (land, peasant).

All these considerations enable one to assume that '*pal^e^ḥîn* of the

House of God' in the edict of Artaxerxes I denotes the non-priestly part of the postexilic community. The content of Ezra 7.24 also agrees with this, although many scholars[1] do interpret this material as a tax exemption only for the priesthood of the Jerusalem temple. More precise is the suggestion of Amusin,[2] who interpreted Ezra 7.24 as a tax exemption for the entire community, which corresponds to the historical situation and politics of Artaxerxes I.

In any case, the inventory of the members of the postexilic community contains no reference to the association of the *n*^e^*tînîm* and the 'sons of the slaves of Solomon' to the postexilic priesthood or temple personnel.

VII

The *nᵉtînîm* are mentioned in the inventory of the builders of the city wall in Jerusalem: 'the *nᵉtînîm* lived in Ophel' (Neh. 3.26; cf. Neh. 11.21). Apart from the remaining socio-professional groups of the postexilic community, who lived throughout the whole community territory,[3] the *nᵉtînîm* formed a compact settlement in Ophel, which recalls the settlement practice of the Palestinian hand workers (e.g. 1 Chron. 4.13-14, 21; Jer. 37.21).[4]

In addition to the above point, there is further evidence in Nehemiah 3, where 'the house of the *nᵉtînîm* and the merchants' (v. 31) is mentioned. The structure of the inventory in Nehemiah 3 proves that collective groups, and individual Jerusalemites, worked on these parts of the wall where they were living in their neighborhoods. If also 'Malchia, son of Haṣorpi... the goldsmiths and merchants' (Neh. 3.31-32) fortified the portion of the wall around the 'house of the *nᵉtînîm*', then they must have lived in close proximity.

Ophel was the oldest part of the city of Jerusalem,[5] the inner fortress where the hand workers and merchants lived in the pre- and postexilic era;[6] and foreigners also lived among them. The royal

1. Meyer, *Die Entstehung*, pp. 65-70; K. Galling, *Studien zur Geschichte Israels im persischen Zeitalter* (1964), pp. 165-78.
2. J.D. Amusin, 'The People of the Land' [Russian], *VDI* 2 (1955), p. 32.
3. Weinberg, 'Demographische Notizen', p. 54.
4. I. Mendelsohn, 'Guilds in Ancient Palestine', *BASOR* 80 (1940), pp. 17-21.
5. B. Mazar, 'Jerusalem' [Hebrew], *EB*, III, p. 794.
6. L. Finkelstein, *The Pharisees: The Sociological Background of their Faith*, I

stamps[1] found in Ophel indicate that apart from their controversial interpretation, people lived in pre-exilic Ophel who were somehow associated with the service of the king of Judah, perhaps in a manner similar to the Ugaritic *bnš mlk.*[2]

Such an assumption also corresponds to the fact that in the onomastica of the *n^e^tînîm* and the 'sons of the slaves of Solomon' one finds names that are derived from indications of a manual worker's profession, for example no. 27 of the *n^e^tînîm* and no. 10 of the 'sons of the slaves of Solomon in Table 2. Noteworthy also are the names with an article (for example, no. 2 of 'sons of the slaves... ' in Table 2) which, according to the views of N. Avigad and J. Naveh,[3] are forms of name-construction indicating the connection of a collective or individual with the royal administration or membership in an association of manual workers.

The foregoing discussion allows one to assume that the *n^e^tînîm* and the 'sons of the slaves of Solomon' lived in Ophel in the pre-exilic times; that they were possibly associated with the royal administration, and were perhaps manual laborers. As such, they were deported (2 Kgs 24.14) while their descendants in the sixth to fifth centuries BCE, because of their social-profession position, stood near the hand workers and merchants who were their neighbours in Ophel.

VIII

Ed. Meyer,[4] who was one of the first to try to deal with the question of the nature of the collectives of the *n^e^tînîm* and the 'sons of the slaves of Solomon', believed that their small numbers proved that they were 'families with few members'. S. Mowinckel,[5] although he recognized the existence of the reduced numbers of the collectives, disagreed, stating that 'the majority of the families (of the *n^e^tînîm* and

(Philadelphia, 1940), pp. 14-16.

1. M.L. Heltzer, 'Ancient Palestinian Ceramic Epigraphy as an Important Historical Source' [Russian], *Epigrafika Vostok* 17 (1966), p. 28.

2. M.L. Heltzer, '"Royal Men" (*bnš mlk*) and the Royal Economic Centres (*gt*) in Ugarit' [Russian], *VDI* 2 (1967), pp. 32-47.

3. N. Avigad, 'A Hebrew Seal with a Family Emblem', *IEJ* 16 (1966), pp. 50-53. J. Naveh, 'Two Hebrew Seals' [Hebrew], *Qadmoniyot* 1 (1968), p. 105.

4. Meyer, *Die Entstehung*, p. 180.

5. Mowinckel, *Studien,* I, p. 79.

the 'sons of the slaves of Solomon') descended from persons dedicated to the temple and, accordingly, were clans'. Also, I.S. Shiffman[1] assumed a gentile organization of the 'sons of the slaves of Solomon'.

The total number of the mature men in 42/45 collectives of the *n^e^tînîm* and the 'sons of the slaves of Solomon' came to 392 (Table 1), which means each collective contained on average nine men. Such a small number of men in the collectives of *n^e^tînîm* and 'sons of the slaves of Solomon' differentiates these groups clearly from the numbers of lay and priestly *bāttê 'ābôt*,[2] as also from the Levites, singers and gatekeepers.

Neh. 11.21 suggests that 'Ziha and Gishpa' had authority over the *n^e^tînîm*. The personal names of both leaders[3] of the *n^e^tînîm* corresponds to the names of the collective no. 1 and perhaps also no. 36 (Table 2). This identification of the personal names of both leaders with the names of two collectives agrees with the previous assumption that the *n^e^tînîm*, as also the 'sons of the slaves of Solomon' were 'family units' in the sixth to fifth centuries BCE. This clearly differentiates the *n^e^tînîm* and the 'sons of the slaves of Solomon' from the other socio-professional groups in the postexilic community, who formed much larger and therefore more powerful agnatic units.

The names of both leaders (Neh. 11.21) and also the whole of the onomastic material indicates a further essential feature of the *n^e^tînîm* and the 'sons of the slaves of Solomon'. As opposed to the lay *bāttê 'ābôt*, priests, and Levites, whose full names contained the individual name, the father's name, and also the name of the collective, the *n^e^tînîm* and the 'sons of the slaves of Solomon' are always referred to with their individual name in the pre- and postexilic periods. Keeping in mind that throughout the ancient Near East fully enfranchised community members are always indicated by individual and father's names and many times also by the names of their community, while those in service are always called only by their names, sometimes with indication of their profession,[4] this is yet further support for our argument.

1. Shiffman, *Legal Status*, p. 57.
2. Weinberg, '*Bēit 'Āḇōt*', pp. 404ff.
3. R.P. Daugerty (*The Shirkutuh*, p. 91) compares the institution of leader of the *n^e^tînîm* with that of the *rab širku* in Babylonia, but there is a closer analogue, that of the *'āb* as the leader of association of craftsmen in Palestine and Ugarit (I. Mendelsohn, *Guilds*, pp. 17-21).
4. I.M. Diakanoff, *The Problems of Property* 4 [Russian], *VDI* 4 (1967), p. 32.

IX

To summarize, this analysis allows the following conclusions:

1. The investigation of the available sources does not support the widely held view that the *n^{e}tînîm* and the 'sons of the slaves of Solomon' belong to the priesthood or temple personnel in the pre- and postexilic periods.

2. It is more likely that in the pre-exilic era the *n^{e}tînîm* and the 'sons of the slaves of Solomon' were hand workers, craftsmen in royal service and/or royal servants who were deported together with other residents of Jerusalem. In the sixth to fifth centuries BCE, both groups belonged to the citizen–temple community. However, the derivation of the royal servants, and the foreign origin of some of the collectives as well as the small numbers (and with that the reduced influence of these collectives), all resulted in the *n^{e}tînîm* and the 'sons of the slaves of Solomon' being assigned the lowest places in the social pyramid, and virtually disappearing after the fifth century BCE.

Chapter 6

THE AGRICULTURAL RELATIONS OF THE CITIZEN–TEMPLE COMMUNITY IN THE ACHAEMENID PERIOD

I

In the study of the Near East in the first millennium BCE, attention has been directed toward the unique socio-political organism which is indicated by the term 'citizen–temple community'. This structure spread extensively in the Achaemenid age, and existed in Asia Minor, Armenia, Mesopotamia, Syria, Phoenicia and Palestine.

The spread of this community structure was conditioned by processes of socio-economic development in the ancient Near East which were also influenced by the evolution of both sectors of the Near East economy, the state and the communal–private sectors.[1] The growth of production and development in a commodity-market economy, the intensification of trade and the active urbanization process lead to the rise of similar individual economies in both of these two sectors. Thanks to this similar economic organization, the representatives of both sectors began to converge (mainly in the towns), which further reduced social differences between them. A separation of individual economies from the state sector took place when their owners joined the temple. The latter, however, became an autonomous and privileged organization of the ruling upper strata during the second half of the second millenium BCE. By merging with the community, the temple formed an essentially new structure—the citizen–temple community. This citizen–temple community gave to its members an organizational unity and a collective self-administration, and took

1. I.M. Diakanoff, *The Main Features of Ancient Society* [Russian]; 'The Problems of Pre-Capitalist Societies in Eastern Countries' (Moscow, 1971), pp. 132-33.

care of political and economic mutual aid.[1]

In the sources concerning the Achaemenid period, the postexilic community of Palestine is the best documented example of the citizen–temple community and therefore this community will serve as a model to reconstruct agricultural relations, although appropriate materials from other citizen–temple communities in the western satrapies will be referred to as well.

II

In contrast to the numerous studies about agricultural relations in pre-exilic Palestine, there are only a few studies about the agrarian structure of the postexilic community. H. Schmidt[2] is of the opinion that the agrarian system institutionalized by Ezra is based on the recognition of Yahweh as the real owner of all property, while the *mišpāḥâ* clan was only the 'renter of the land of God'. Schmidt refers to the ancient roots of this agrarian system, but he notices that 'the law (the property law of Ezra) obviously did not prove to be very long-lasting'. The assumption of a law of property expounded by Ezra is disputable and Schmidt's concept does not reveal the actual nature of agricultural relations in the postexilic community.

According to Kreissig,[3] clan property was already gradually becoming the possession of the privileged upper classes in the first half of the first millennium BCE. The deportation of the Judaean upper strata by the Babylonians advanced the independence of farmers who were no longer dependent on property owners. In Achaemenid Judah, the private possession of land was predominantly in the form of small rural properties, as well as in the form of large estates owned by the Persian kings, the governors in Judah, other officials and the heads of the rich families. Land as the property of communities or clans is not attested. H. Kreissig's concept is stimulating, but it is not the only possible solution to this difficult problem.[4]

1. Diakanoff, *The Main Features*, p. 133.

2. H. Schmidt, *Das Bodenrecht im Verfassungsentwurf des Esra* (Halle, 1932), pp. 8-19.

3. H. Kreissig, *Die sozialökonomische Situation in Juda zur Achämenidenzeit* (Berlin, 1973), pp. 23-38, 77-86.

4. On a more detailed examination of Kreissig's concept: J.P. Weinberg, 'Probleme der sozialökonomischen Struktur Judas vom 6. Jh. v.u.Z. bis zum 1. Jh.

III

A detailed study of the agricultural relations of pre-exilic Palestine would exceed the limits of this study, but a short survey is useful because it can help us to understand the agricultural relations of the postexilic community.

Noth's[1] opinion that Samarian ostraca of the ninth century BCE were letters about the delivery of the produce of the royal estates was disputed by Aharoni and Rainey.[2] They were of the opinion that those ostraca were letters about the delivery of produce from the population to the royal storehouses. The determination of the *lmlk*-stamp[3] is also disputed, because some scholars[4] argue that these vessels were used for the delivery of taxes-in-kind in the Judaean state, while others[5] assume that these stamps simply serve to indicate that the vessels were produced in royal kilns. Some scholars[6] are of the opinion that these stamps prove the existence of royal estates, grain fields and vineyards. Old Testament texts (e.g. 1 Sam. 8.12; 1 Chron. 27.25-31), and 'the reaper's complaint' from Meṣad Hashavyahu,[7] as well as other data,

v.u.Z.', *Jahrbuch für Wirtschaftsgeschichte* (1973), pp. 237-51.

1. M. Noth, 'Das Krongut der israelitischen Könige und seine Verwaltung', *ZDPV* 50 (1927), pp. 219ff.

2. Y. Aharoni, 'The Samaria Ostraca—an Additional Note', *IEJ* 12 (1962), pp. 67-69; A.F. Rainey, 'Administration in Ugarit and the Samaria Ostraca', *IEJ* 12 (1962), pp. 62-63; Rainey, 'The Samaria Ostraca in the Light of Fresh Evidence', *PEQ* (1967), pp. 32-41; Rainey, 'Semantic Parallels to the Samaria Ostraca', *PEQ* (1970), pp. 45-51.

3. H.D. Lance, 'The Royal Israelite Stamps and the Kingdom of Judah', *HTR* 64 (1971), pp. 315-32; A.D. Tushingham, 'A Royal Israelite Seal and the Royal Jar Handle Stamps', *BASOR* 200 (1970), pp. 71-78; 201 (1971), pp. 23-35; P. Welten, *Die Königs-Stempel: Ein Beitrag zur Militärpolitik Judas unter Hiskia und Josia* (Wiesbaden, 1969).

4. Y. Aharoni, *Excavations at Ramat-Rahel (Seasons 1959 and 1960)* (Rome, 1962), pp. 51-56; Y. Aharoni, 'Report on the Beer-Sheba Expedition: Notes and News', *PEQ* (1971), pp. 64-66; W.F. Albright, *The Excavation of Tell Beit Mirsim: III The Iron Age* (AASOR, 11-12; New Haven, 1943), pp. 74-75; Welten, *Die Königs-Stempel*.

5. M.L. Heltzer, 'Ancient Palestinian Ceramic Epigraphy as an Important Historical Source' [Russian], *Epigraphica Vostoka* 17 (1966), p. 36.

6. F.M. Cross, Jr, 'Judean Stamps', *E-I* 9 (1969), pp. 20-22; O. Tufnell, *Lachish III (Tell ed-Duweir): The Iron Age* (London, 1953), pp. 105-28, 312-17.

7. J.D. Amusin and M.L. Heltzer, 'The Inscriptions from Mezad Hashavyahu',

permit us to assume that royal domains existed in pre-exilic Judah, but that the Davidic house was not the main owner of all the land.[1]

The problem of temple land in pre-exilic Palestine is more difficult. Nevertheless, it is possible to suggest that some of the pre-exilic Yahwistic temples and sanctuaries might have had their own land and economy. For such an assumption, which Henry[2] once argued, the following arguments seem relevant:

1. In the countries adjoining Palestine, in the second millennium BCE as well as in the first part of the first millennium BCE, temple land and temple estates were structural elements of their economy. This applies also to Canaanite cultural settings,[3] whose considerable influence on pre-exilic Israelite society is no longer in doubt. The Egyptian temples in Palestine in the second half of the second millennium BCE owned land and operated economies.[4]

2. The Old Testament aetiological legends about the foundation of several sanctuaries or the 'divine promise oaths'[5] prove that there often had been a purchase of land by the patriarch-founders (Gen. 33.18-20), or the patriarchs at least put up a tent on the land of the future sanctuary (Gen. 12.6-8) before the foundation of the sanctuary. Perhaps the vineyards in Shiloh, where the Shilonite girls were dancing on 'Yahweh's feast day' (Judg. 21.19ff.) were the property of the local sanctuary?[6]

3. In Horst's[7] opinion, the term '*naḥ*^{a}*lâ* of Yahweh' often describes

[Russian] *VDI* 3 (1963), pp. 118-25.

1. I.Sh. Shiffman, *The Agrarian System in the First Half of the First Millennium BCE*, p. 41.

2. K.H. Henry, 'Land Tenure in the Old Testament', *PEQ* (1954), pp. 5-15; Kreissig, *Die sozialökonomische Situation*, pp. 25-26.

3. W.F. Albright, 'Some Canaanite-Phoenician Sources of Hebrew Wisdom', *Wisdom in Israel and in the Ancient Near East* (VTSup, 3; Leiden, 1955), pp. 1-3 ; K.-H. Bernhardt, *Das Problem der altorientalischen Königsideologie* (VTSup, 8; Leiden, 1961), pp. 102ff.

4. A. Alt, 'Ägyptische Tempel in Palästina und die Landnahme der Philister', *KSGVI*, I, pp. 216-30.

5. F.W. Golka, 'Zur Erforschung der Ätiologien im Alten Testament', *VT* 20 (1970) pp. 90-98; H.C. White, 'The Divine Oath in Genesis', *JBL* 92 (1973), pp. 165-79.

6. H.H. Rowley, *Worship in Ancient Israel* (London, 1967), p. 104.

7. F. Horst, 'Zwei Begriffe für Eigentum (Besitz)', *Verbannung und Heimkehr: Beiträge zur Geschichte und Theologie Israels im 6. und 5. Jh. v. Chr.* (Tübingen,

Mt Moriah where Yahweh's temple was located (Exod. 15.17; Ps. 79.1).

4. The report about buying the 'threshing floor of Aravna', noted that the price paid by David was 50 shekels (2 Sam. 24.24). This report, according to Mazar,[1] was about land of the Jerusalem divinity Sedek[2] (2 Sam. 24.18-25; 1 Chron. 21.18-26). But the price is what is particularly interesting. Although the Near East was known for its price fluctuations, very low prices for land (except Ugarit) can be found. In Arrapha the price of one *iku* (0.35 ha) was 12 shekels, in Kassitian Babylonia 12.4 shekels and in the Hittite empire only 1–3 shekels.[3] The reason for such low prices was that, in most cases, the land was sold under pressure by the purchaser. The same happened in the case of the 'threshing floor of Araunah', because David was the victor over a defeated Jerusalem. If these considerations are legitimate, the 'threshing floor of Araunah' would have been significantly larger than the later temple of Solomon.[4]

5. In Jeremiah 7, the prophet preached the destruction of the temple saying: 'My anger and my wrath shall be poured out on this place, on human beings and animals, on the trees of the field and the fruit of the ground; it will burn and not be quenched' (v. 20). The crux of this sentence is the word *māqôm*, which in Deuteronomy (12.14, 21) describes Yahweh's central sanctuary[5] and which alternates with the terms '*hêkāl* of Yahweh' and '*bêt* of Yahweh' (Jer. 7. 2, 4) in this chapter. This points, without a doubt, to the temple of Jerusalem.[6] In the Old Testament, the word *'ādām* was not generally used as a designation for priests, therefore it is not impossible that the mention of people and cattle, trees and fruits, meant that the *māqôm hazzeh*, the

1961), pp. 141-43.

1. B. Mazar, 'Jerusalem—The Temple of the King and the House of the Kingdom', in *Judah and Jerusalem* [Hebrew] (Jerusalem, 1957), pp. 27-29.

2. R.A. Rosenberg, 'The God Ṣedeq', *HUCA* 36 (1965), pp. 161-77.

3. M.L. Heltzer, 'Commodities and Prices in the Trade of Ancient Ugarit' [Russian], *PS* 19 (1919), p. 30.

4. Th.A. Busink, *Der Tempel von Jerusalem von Salomo bis Herodes*, I (Leiden, 1970), pp. 162-352.

5. W. Staerk, 'Noch einmal das Problem des Deuteronomiums', *Beiträge zur Religionsgeschichte und Archäologie Palästinas* (Leipzig, 1927), pp. 139-50.

6. K.D. Schunk, 'Zentralheiligtum, Grenzheiligtum und Jahweheiligtum', *Numen* 18 (1971), pp. 132-40; P. Welten, 'Kulthöhe und Jahwetempel', *ZDPV* 88 (1972), pp. 19-37.

Jerusalem temple, had its own economy.

These arguments should not be regarded as a final proof for the existence of temple lands and a temple economy in Jerusalem. But if closer inspection confirms our hypothesis, at the same time it will prove that the temple land belonged to the state sector of the economy.[1] This is because the pre-exilic Yahwistic temple, especially the Jerusalem temple, was very closely connected with the state.[2]

In the system of agricultural relations in pre-exilic Palestine, the 48 Levitical towns are important. The arguments of those who dispute the existence of these towns are not convincing, and considerable support can be cited for the existence of these Levitical towns in the first half of the first millennium BCE.[3] In the opinion of Mazar, Haran, and Horst, the Levites only owned houses and grazing land in the towns mentioned, but the fields were the property of the local inhabitants—the non-Levites. The analysis of the terms *śᵉdê migrāš* and *migrāš*, which describe Levitical land (e.g. Lev. 25.34; Num. 35.3; Josh. 14.4; 2 Chron. 31.19) also allows another interpretation. The word *śādeh* appears about 310 times in the Old Testament and often (about 50 times) describes 'ploughed and sowed fields' (e.g. Gen. 30.14; Exod. 22.5; Ruth 2.2, 3).

Migrāš is only mentioned five times (out of c. 110 times) without any connection to Levitical towns, and describes in those cases (e.g. Ezek. 36.5; 45.2; 48.15, 17) a 'vicinity of the town'. Sometimes, mainly when it is talking about the Levitical towns in the Negeb or other cattle breeding areas in Palestine, *migrāš* is a designation of grazing land. But in other cases *migrāš* means 'vicinity of the town' and *śᵉdê migrāš*—'farming land in the vicinity of the town' where the Levites cultivated grain and grapes—corresponding to the economic characteristic of the region.

Gunneweg and Strauss[4] are of the opinion that *śᵉdê migrāš* was 'a

1. Diakanoff, *Main Features*, pp. 132-33.

2. Mazar, *Jerusalem*, pp. 27-29; Schunck, 'Zentralheiligtum', pp. 132-40; Welten, 'Kulthöhe', pp. 35-37.

3. W.F. Albright, 'The List of Levitical Cities', *Louis Ginzberg Jubilee*, I (New York, 1945), pp. 49-73; A. Alt, 'Festungen und Levitenorte im Lande Juda', *KSGVI*, II, pp. 306-15; B. Mazar, 'The Cities of the Priests and the Levites', *VTSup* 7 (1960), pp. 193-205.

4. A.H.J. Gunneweg, *Leviten und Priester* (Göttingen, 1965), p. 65; H. Strauss, *Untersuchungen zu den Überlieferungen der vorexilischen Leviten* (Bonn, 1960), p. 134.

kind of loan and fief within the local community'. Haran[1] states that the *migrāš* which were allocated to the Levites that, did not become their property, and he supports this by noting the opposition of *migrāš*—*'ᵃḥuzzâ* in Ezek. 45.6 and 48.16-18. But Haran's reference to Ezekiel argues against him, because the term *migrāš* is used in Ezek. 48.16-18, where a quantative assessment of the area of Jerusalem is given, while in Ezek. 45.6 the term *'ᵃḥuzzâ* is mentioned where special attention is given to the religious/juridical status of the same region. The terms *migrāš* and *śᵉdê migrāš* on the one hand, and *'ᵃḥuzzâ* and *naḥᵃlâ* on the other hand, are on different descriptive levels. The first ones express the economic characteristics of the property, while the second ones point to the proper status of the ground.

In Hirschberg's opinion,[2] *'ᵃḥuzzâ* is property of the individual, or the community and can only be bequeathed within the community. Horst[3] suggests that there would be two terms for the description of the property right in the Old Testament—*naḥᵃlâ* and *'ᵃḥuzzâ*, which are very close in their contents, but *'ᵃḥuzzâ* would be the more general, legal, abstract term, compared to the other term, *naḥᵃlâ*. Shiffman[4] accepts the similarity of both terms, but the research of Amusin, de Vaux and others[5] proves that in pre-exilic Palestine there was a principle inalienability of the property of the laity and priestly agnatic collectives—the *'ᵃḥuzzâ*/*naḥᵃlâ*.

Thus, the system of agricultural relations in pre-exilic Palestine included the royal estates, and possibly temple lands which formed the state sector of the economy, and the *'ᵃḥuzzâ*/*naḥᵃlâ* of the laity and priests, which belonged to the private–communal sector of economy.

IV

The conquest of Judah by the Babylonians and the deportation of a part of the inhabitants caused substantial changes in agricultural relations. But note that only about 10% of the inhabitants of Judah—the royal court, the inhabitants of the capital, the majority of the Judaean

1. M. Haran, 'The Towns of the Levites: Utopia and Historical Reality' [Hebrew], *Tarbiz* 27 (1958), p. 425.
2. Ch.Z. Hirschberg, "'ᵃḥuzzâ' [Hebrew], *EB*, I, pp. 209-10.
3. Horst, 'Zwei Begriffe', pp. 135-56.
4. Shiffman, *Agrarian System*, pp. 34-35.
5. J.D. Amusin, 'The People of the Land' [Russian], *VDI* 2 (1957), pp. 16ff.

nobility and a part of the Judaean *'am hā'āreṣ* were deported, while those without property in the south, as well as almost the whole population in the north of Judah, remained.[1]

In the development of the neo-Assyrian and neo-Babylonian world empires, a great part of the land in the conquered countries, mainly the property of the state sector, and the land of the deported people, became the property of the victorious kings. In the places where the neo-Assyrian and the neo-Babylonian rulers settled local and deported people, these were looked upon as 'slaves on the ground'. Such people were organized in secondary communities, who owned a certain property, paid taxes and so on.[2] One may assume that the agrarian changes (2 Kgs 25.12 = Jer. 52.16; Jer. 39.10) carried out by the Babylonians in Judah were of the same nature.

Important although controversial evidence for this exists in epigraphical material in Engedi.[3] This flourishing centre of perfume production was the property of the Judaean kings in the seventh to sixth centuries BCE (1 Chron. 4.23). On one jug-handle[4] there is a mark with four letters from the sixth century BCE. The first and third letters are undoubtedly read as *lamed* and *'aleph*, but the second and fourth can be read as *nun* and *mem*, or *tav* and *'aleph*. Yeivin suggests the reading *l^e^mārê*. The Aramaic word *mare* is frequently used as a king's title, or address formula in the Old Testament (e.g. Dan. 2.47; 4.16) and in the epigraphical material. If Yeivin's way of reading is the right one, the inscription reads as '(Belonging) to the master', which in Babylonian Judah could only refer to the Babylonian king, who probably was the owner of Engedi.

There is other evidence confirming such an interpretation of the changes of property relations implemented by the Babylonians. In Assyrian sources people settled on royal ground are named after their professions—'farmer', 'vine-grower', and so on.[5] The same

1. J.P. Weinberg, 'Demographische Notizen zur Geschichte der nachexilischen Gemeinde in Juda', *Klio* 54 (1972), pp. 46-50.

2. I.M. Diakonoff, *The Development of Agrarian Relations in Assyria* [Russian] (Leningrad, 1949), pp. 90ff.; and in *Main Economic Features*, p. 133; V.A. Jacobsen, 'The Social Structure of the Neo-Assyrian State' [Russian], *VDI* 1 (1965), pp. 114ff.

3. B. Mazar, 'En-Gedi', *'Atiqot* 5, 21 (1966), pp. 34-35; 'Excavations at the Oasis of Engedi', *Archaeology* 16 (1963), pp. 101-104.

4. B. Mazar, 'En-Gedi', p. 34, n. 12, pl. 26, 1.

5. Diakanoff, *Development*, p. 111.

designation is given in the Old Testament to those of the *dallat ʿam hāʾāreṣ* who after 586 BCE were given land by the Babylonian conquerors. The distribution of property to the *dallat ʿam* is expressed with the verb *ntn* (Jer. 39.10) which can also mean 'to lend'.[1] It is entirely possible that the small settlements attributed to the Babylonian era, which were detected in Bethlehem and in other places, were inhabited by *dallat ʿam hāʾāreṣ*.[2]

Babylonian supremacy caused important changes in the system of property relations, mainly in southern Judah. But those changes did not lead to a reinforcement of private property but to a colossal growth of the state sector. Since that sector belonged to a foreign and detested supreme power, a large part of the local non-deported population of Judah tried to separate from it, which also corresponds to the expectations of the exiles in Mesopotamia.

V

Before looking at the agrarian relations of the postexilic citizen–temple community, one should mention that this community included only a part of the territory and population of Achaemenid Judah. The data in Ezra and Nehemiah point to the persistent efforts of the lay and priestly *bāttê ʾābôt* to return to the towns which had been occupied by their ancestors. Epigraphical data also support this. In pre-exilic Engedi, there is a seal with the inscription, '(Belonging) to Uriyahu, (son) of Azaryahu'.[3] But there is also a seal with the name Uriah in the large residential building (no. 234) of the postexilic era.[4] The occurrence of the relatively rare name Uriyahu = Uriah in pre- and postexilic Engedi is hardly an accident. Similarly, in Arad in the pre-exilic temple an ostracon was found with the name Mermot,[5] a name which repeatedly occurs on ostraca from Achaemenid Arad.[6] Meremot is not a common name and its occurrence in pre- and

1. F.I. Andersen, 'The Socio-Juridical Background of the Naboth Incident', *JBL* 85 (1966), pp. 46-57.

2. J.P. Weinberg, 'Postexilic Palestine: An Archaeological Report', *Proceedings of the Israel Academy of Sciences and the Humanities* 4 (1971), p. 20.

3. B. Mazar, 'En-Gedi', p. 20, tables 26, 30.

4. B. Mazar and I. Dunayevsky, *Yediot* 30 (1966), p. 183.

5. Y. Aharoni, *IEJ* 14.4 (1964), p. 282.

6. Y. Aharoni, *IEJ* 15.4 (1964), pp. 250-51.

postexilic Arad confirms the assumption that *bāttê 'ābôt* whose ancestors occupied Engedi, Arad and other villages in the pre-exilic period, returned to their towns. This effort of the postexilic *bāttê 'ābôt* is most probably connected with the desire to win back their lost *'^{a}ḥuzzâ/naḥ^{a}lâ*. In Neh. 11.3 (= 1 Chron. 9.2) we are told that, 'in the towns of Judah, each man lived on his own *'^{a}ḥuzzâ*', but 17 lines further we can read that, 'priests and Levites made their homes throughout the towns of Judah, each man on his own *naḥ^{a}lâ* (v. 20).' In both cases they are members of the citizen–temple community, but the question remains as to whether the terms *'^{a}ḥuzzâ/naḥ^{a}lâ* kept their earlier meaning, or if in the context of the Achaemenid changes the old meanings took on a new content.

Boaz confirms his willingness to fulfil the *g^{e}'ullâ*-obligation in front of witnesses: 'Today you are witnesses, that I have bought everything that had been Elimelek's...so that I raise the deceased's name on his *naḥ^{a}lâ*' (Ruth 4.9-10). The *g^{e}'ullâ*-duty has its roots in the principle of inalienability of property, and the *naḥ^{a}lâ* of the book of Ruth is ground which can only be sold within the agnatic community. Judith did not have direct heirs, therefore she distributed her property between her husband's relatives and the members of her clan (Jdt. 16.24). That means she acted according to the rule that property has to stay within the agnatic community. These arguments allow the conclusion that the terms *'^{a}ḥuzzâ/naḥ^{a}lâ* described the property of the *bāttê 'ābôt* of the sixth to fourth centuries BCE. In the second half of the fifth century BCE the influential priestly *bêt 'ābôt* of Pashḥur (Neh. 11.21 = 1 Chron. 9.12) lived in Jerusalem, at whose head stood a certain Adaiah, but a seal with the following inscription was found in the surroundings of Jerusalem: '(Belonging) to Pashḥur, the son of Adayahu'. One of the Pashḥurides has the rare name Ishmael (Ezra 10.22) which occurs on one of the seals found in Jerusalem. Also the seal with the following inscription should be taken into account, '(Belonging) to Adata, wife of Pashḥur'. Thus, we have maybe four seals of the members of one *bêt 'ābôt*, and the fact that three of them have been found in the surroundings of Jerusalem allows the assumption that the Pashḥurides' *'^{a}ḥuzzâ/naḥ^{a}lâ* was located there.

Of most interest is the Aramaic ostracon from the middle of the fifth century BCE from Tell el-Fara':[1] 'For the sowing in the near/ field

1. E. Stern, 'The Land of Israel in the Persian Period' [Hebrew], *Qadmoniyot* 2.4 (1969), p. 112.

rate 3 *k(orim)* in the *'ᵃḥuzzâ k(orim)* 35' (*kor* is a measure of grain equal to approximately 359 litres).

This ostracon from Tell el-Fara' is the only document of this kind to be found in the area of a citizen–temple community and therefore hasty conclusions must be avoided. But this ostracon confirms our interpretation of *śādeh* and allows the assumption that the 'near field' belonged to the *'ᵃḥuzzâ*. In Mesopotamia, the seed use was about 55–85 litres per hectare (according to Klima)[1] or about 112.5 litres per hectare (according to Dandamaev)[2] in the first millennium BCE. If the seed use in Palestine was similar to this, there would be an area of about 111–228 ha. for the *'ᵃḥuzzâ* and an area of about 9.5–19.6 ha. for the field.

These are only speculations, of course, and there is more reason to assume that the *'ᵃḥuzzâ/naḥᵃlâ* of the *bêt 'ābôt* was divided in parcels, which were the property of families belonging to the *bêt 'ābôt*. This would also clarify the conflict within the citizen–temple community caused by usury, the concentration of property and serfdom in the middle of the fifth century BCE (Nehemiah 5). The victims of this concentration of property and serfdom are described with the term *'āḥ* (e.g. Neh. 5.7, 8) which is mentioned about 35 times in Ezra–Nehemiah and mostly describes an individual's membership of the *bêt 'ābôt*.[3] The *'aḥîm* were members of the *bêt 'ābôt* and the wealthy and influential families within these collectives seized a part of the parcels of land in the middle of the fifth century BCE. Such a process of concentration of land and slavery by the community members and the unavoidable intensification of social conflict was extremely dangerous for the citizen–temple community, surrounded as it was by enemies.[4] Therefore, Nehemiah used the old law of the *šᵉmiṭṭâ* (Lev. 25.11-13; Deut. 15.1-3),[5] which has its roots in the principle of inalienability of the common property, as well as the related principle of mutual support.

1. J. Klima, *Gesellschaft und Kultur des alten Mesopotamien* (Prague, 1964), p. 122.

2. Personal communication from M.A. Dandamaev, for which I am very grateful.

3. J.P. Weinberg, 'Das *Bēit 'Āḇōt* im 6–4 Jh. v.u.Z.', *VT* 23, 4 (1973), p. 408.

4. J.P. Weinberg, 'Der *'am hā'āreṣ* des 6–4 Jh. v.u.Z.', *Klio* 56 (1974), pp. 235-335.

5. J. Lewy, 'The Biblical Institution of *Deror* in the Light of Akkadian Documents', *E-I* 5 (1958), pp. 21-31; Sh. Loewenstamm, '*yōḇēl*' [Hebrew], *EB*, III, pp. 578-81.

This contradicts the view that private property dominated in postexilic Judah. Support for private property is found in the Samarian papyri,[1] but these data do not refer to the citizen–temple community, but to the province Shomron (Samaria).

The land of the postexilic citizen–temple community was formally accepted as Yahweh's property (Neh. 9.8, 36) but in the sixth to fourth centuries BCE the Jerusalem temple owned no land and did not have its own economy. The land was de facto inalienable property, the *'ᵃḥuzzâ/naḥᵃlâ* of the *bêt 'ābôt*, and was divided into parcels, which in turn were the possession of the families within the *bêt 'ābôt*. How does the agrarian system of the Palestinian citizen–temple community compare with agrarian relations in the other citizen–temple communities in the Achaemenid Near East?

VI

The work of Dandamaev,[2] Sarkisian[3] and Perichanian[4] proved that the relevant deity was accepted as the supreme 'owner' of all the land in all the citizen–temple communities of the Achaemenid era in Mesopotamia, Asia Minor and Armenia. But the recognition was mostly of an abstract and conventional nature, because all the land, or the majority of it, was in reality used by all the members of the citizen–temple community.

Besides these basic features that were common to all citizen–temple communities, there were important differences. In the sixth to fourth centuries BCE, the agricultural relations of the citizen–temple communities diverged along two lines: (A) the existence, or nonexistence of temple property, and (B) the existence or nonexistence of temple economies. All citizen–temple communities of the Achaemenid period can be divided into three groups:

1. F.M. Cross, Jr, 'The Discovery of the Samaria Papyri', *BA* 26 (1963), pp. 115-16.

2. M.A. Dandamaev, 'The Temple Tithe in Late Babylonia' [Russian], *VDI* 2 (1965), pp. 14-34; and 'Temple and State', pp. 17-39.

3. G.Ch. Sarkisian, 'Self-Governing Town in Seleucid Babylonia' [Russian], *VDI* 4 (1966), pp. 68-83; and 'On City-Land in Seleucid Babylonia' [Russian], *VDI* 1 (1953), pp. 59-73.

4. A.G. Perichanian, *The Temple Communities of Asia Minor and Armenia* [Russian] (Moscow, 1959).

A1. Those communities whose temples were *de facto* owners of the land. The temples partly leased this land to community members, and partly organized their own economies (Uruk, Sippar, Comana).

A2. Those communities whose temples were *de facto* owners of the land but who did not organize their own economies and left all the temple-land for the use of the community members (Mylasa-Olymos and others).

B. Those communities whose temples did not own land nor operate their own economy. A typical representative of this group was the Jerusalem citizen–temple community.

The reasons for such cardinal differences cannot be discussed in this essay. Therefore, it should only be remarked that these distinctions determined the structure of temple personnel and temple income, and the role of the temple in the given community.

The study of agricultural relations in the citizen–temple community of the Achaemenid age has to be continued, as it is of basic importance in comprehending the structures of world empires in the first millennium BCE.

Chapter 7

CENTRAL AND LOCAL ADMINISTRATION IN THE ACHAEMENID EMPIRE

I

In the historic development of the Near East, the first millennium BCE occupies a special place, distinguished from the previous millennium particularly by the structure of society and economics, politics and culture.[1] A striking characteristic of the first millennium BCE is the so-called 'world empire', for example the neo-Assyrian, the neo-Babylonian and the Achaemenid.[2] Among these empires, the relationship between central and local power is of particular importance.

This issue has occupied the interest of many scholars[3] who discuss this internal relationship within different world empires, including the Achaemenid. Scholars have previously outlined the organization of the Achaemenid world empire with its highly developed and complex structure of central and local power, and frequently one reads views such as 'the Persian political structure is similar to early Roman development...'

The relationship is particularly complicated and multifaceted between the central power on the one side—that is, the central bureaucratic administration with its local organs (for example, satrap and satrapy,

1. I.M. Diakanoff, 'The Main Economic Features of the Monarchies of Ancient Western Asia' [Russian], *NAA* 1 (1966), pp. 44-58; *Main Features of Ancient Society* [Russian], 'The Problems of Pre-Capitalist Societies in Asian Countries' (Moscow, 1971), pp. 142-43.

2. N.B. Jankovskaya, 'Some Aspects of Economy of the Assyrian Empire' [Russian], *VDI* 1 (1956), pp. 28-46; Diakanoff, *Main Features*, pp. 133-34.

3. For example, M. Dandamaev, 'Politische und wirtschaftliche Geschichte', in G. Walser (ed.), *Beiträge zur Achämenidengeschichte* (Hesperia Einzelschriften, 18; 1972), pp. 18-27.

peḥâ and provinces), and the self-governing institutions within the satrapies and provinces on the other side. The term 'local administration' is used in this study to designate only the autonomous structures whose forms were quite varied in the Achaemenid empire.

The polis of Asia Minor, the Phoenician city, the principalities of Caria and Paphlagonia, the tribes of the Colchians, Arabs, and others, all belonged to the 'local administration', but the outstanding and most significant type of autonomous self-government in the sixth century BCE was the 'citizen–temple community' in Babylonia, Syria, Asia Minor, Armenia, Phoenicia and Palestine. Therefore, the relationship between the Achaemenid central administration and the citizen–temple community, as the most important form of self-administration, should be investigated in detail.[1]

The most well-documented source for the Achaemenid period is the postexilic community of Judah, so this serves as a model for the solution of the task set before us. Notably, the postexilic community is an outstanding example of the citizen–temple community,[2] and thus can be referred to for conclusions about this type of 'local administration', with, however, certain reservations. Furthermore, the sources about the history of the postexilic community allow one to analyse the 200-year evolution of the relationship of 'central' and 'local' administration, which is not possible for other citizen–temple communities.

Modern biblical studies considers the origin of the postexilic community in Judah to be mainly the result of an internal development of the people and Yahweh-worship,[3] or the 'product of the Persian

1. Some aspects of these problems are already considered by M.A. Dandamaev, 'Temple and State in Late Babylonia' [Russian], *VDI* 4 (1966), pp. 17-35; A.G. Perichanian, *The Temple Communities of Asia Minor and Armenia* (Moscow, 1959), pp. 143-69.

2. On the essence of the citizen–temple community, see J.P. Weinberg, *The Citizen–Temple Community in the Western Provinces of the Achaemenid Empire* [Russian] (Tbilisi, 1973).

3. This concept, inspired by J. Wellhausen, *Prolegomena zur Geschichte Israels* (Berlin, 1927), was later modified in certain details by A.C. Welch, in 'The Share of North-Israel in the Restoration of the Temple Worship', *ZAW* 7 (48) (1939), p. 175; A. Bentzen, 'Priesterschaft und Laien in der jüdischen Gemeinde des fünften Jahrhunderts', *AfO* 6 (1931), pp. 280-86; J. Liver, *The Time of Ezra and Nehemiah* [Hebrew], pp. 6-8; J. Klausner, *The History of the Second Temple*, I [Hebrew] (Jerusalem, 1954), pp. 14-17; M. Noth, *Geschichte Israels* (Göttingen, 1956), p. 267; H.H. Guthrie, Jr, *God and History in the Old Testament* (Greenwich, 1960),

empire'.[1] Both views portray the postexilic community as a unique historical religious phenomenon and stress only one cause of the genesis of the community. Decisive for the development and growth of all citizen–temple communities, including the Palestinian one, was the process of socio-economic development of the Near East at the beginning of the first millennium BCE and the evolution of the two sectors of the Near Eastern economy—the state and private–communal sector.[2] But other important and complicated causes for the genesis of the citizen–temple community cannot be ignored, especially the specific consequences of the entire system of relationships between the 'central' and 'local' administration in the Achaemenid Empire, the chronologically and geographically variable attitude of the Persian central administration to different citizen–temple communities, and also the subjective individual aspirations of the citizen–temple communities themselves.

II

The emergence of the state is the result of the impact of socio-economic development, but one should not overlook subjective factors, especially in the cases of secondary political structures, that is, in the efforts of a destroyed political existence to rebuild again. In such situations (*Nullpunkten*),[3] the attitude of different social circles and powers to the former state, and the notions about the desired future state play a significant rôle.

This is confirmed by the different plans of restoration which were outlined after the disaster of 586 BCE among both the exiles, and those

pp. 92-96; K. Galling, *Studien zur Geschichte Israels im persischen Zeitalter* (Tübingen, 1964), p. 148; P.R. Ackroyd, *Exile and Restoration: A Study of Hebrew Thought of the Sixth Century BC* (London, 1968).

1. Prominent among those who hold to this opinion of E. Meyer (*Die Entstehung des Judentums* [Halle, 1896], pp. 4-5, 70-72) are: Y. Kaufmann, 'Probleme der israelitisch-jüdischen Religionsgeschichte', *ZAW* 7 (1930), pp. 23-43; B. Mazar, 'The Land of Israel' [Hebrew], *EB*, I, pp. 736–37; L. Rost, 'Erwägungen zum Kyroserlass', *VuH*, pp. 302-304.

2. Diakanoff, *Main Features*, pp. 132-39; J.P. Weinberg, 'Agrarverhältnisse in der Bürger-Tempel-Gemeinde der Achämenidenzeit', *AAASH* 2 (1974), pp. 473–74.

3. This expression was suggested by W. Zimmerli, in 'Planungen für den Wiederaufbau nach der Katastrophe von 587', *VT* 18 (1968), p. 229.

who remained behind. There is much to be said for the view of Welch, Guthrie, Janssen, and others, that the *Sitz im Leben* of Lamentations, Obadiah, many parts of Jeremiah and some Psalms, is to be found amongst those left in the land,[1] where according to Pfeiffer, Noth, Lebram, and Janssen *et al.* the Deuteronomic History is also located.[2] If such views are correct, then these texts must contain thoughts about the future of the people and prophecies about the coming state, and so forth. Indeed, the hope for the rebuilding of the temple is spoken of, as is the return of the exiles and the renewal of the Davidic Kingdom (e.g. Jer. 23.5-8; Lam. 4.22). But these writers of restoration plans do not seek to renew the old existence in all aspects. With the lasting impact of the catastrophe and the exile, and with the guilt of the Davidic dynasty, there is a limitation of the power of the future king. It appears that the restoration plan of the population that was not deported from Judah envisions a re-establishment of an ideal Davidic monarchy.

The exiles were also concerned with the future, since it was in their midst that a restoration plan involving the so-called *nāśî* stratum develops.[3] This plan which was developed in the second half of the sixth century BCE (in any case before 515), envisioned the re-establishment of a state in Palestine with a *nāśî* at the head (e.g. Ezek. 45.16-17; 46.4, 16, 17). According to Rautenberg, North, Klausner, Macholz and others, this plan foresees the establishment of a theocracy,[4] while other scholars[5] are of the opinion that the plan envisions the restoration

1. Welch, *Share*, pp. 175-87; Guthrie, *God*, pp. 92-95; E. Janssen, *Juda in der Exilszeit* (FRLANT, 51/69; Göttingen, 1956), pp. 82-94.

2. R.H. Pfeiffer, *Introduction to the Old Testament* (New York, 1941), pp. 365-68; M. Noth, *Überlieferungsgeschichtliche Studien*, I (Königsberg, 1942), pp. 97-108; Janssen, 'Juda', *Exilszeit*, pp. 82-94; J.C.H. Lebram, 'Nachbiblische Weisheitstraditionen', *VT* 15 (1965), p. 228.

3. H. Gese, *Der Verfassungsentwurf des Ezechiel (Kap. 40–48) traditionsgeschichtlich untersucht* (Tübingen, 1957), pp. 85-88, 110-11.

4. W. Rautenberg, 'Zur Zukunftsthora des Hesekiel', *ZAW* 33 (1913), pp. 105-107; C.R. North, 'The Religious Aspects of Hebrew Kingship', *ZAW* 9 (50) (1932), p. 19; Klausner, *History*, I, pp. 11-12; G.Ch. Macholz, 'Noch einmal: Planungen für den Wiederaufbau nach der Katastrophe von 587', *VT* 19 (1969), pp. 336-43.

5. G.A. Cooke, 'Some Considerations on the Text and Teaching of Ezekiel 40–48', *ZAW* 1 (42) (1924), pp. 114-15; Gese, *Der Verfassungsentwurf*, pp. 116-19; Zimmerli, 'Planungen', pp. 244-46; Sh. Talmon, 'The "Desert Motif" in the Bible

of the monarchy, but with a *nāśî* in the place of the traditional *melek*. Mainly in Ezekiel 1–39, the term *nāśî*, in contrast to *melek*, means 'the head of a major political power and lesser foreign rulers'.[1] Within Israel, stated Noth, Buccellati and others,[2] the use of the term indicates that the *nāśî* was a leader of the tribe and its representative in the council of the so-called Amphictiony of the 12 tribes, but according to Speiser[3] *nāśî* was the head of the *bêt 'āb*, and as such he could be 'tribal leader' and 'head of a combination or confederation of a number of tribes'. In any case, the term *nāśî* is rooted in the ancient tribal tradition, and the restoration plan in the *nāśî* stratum aimed not toward an establishment of a theocracy or restoration of the Davidic monarchy, but toward the formation of something like the tribal organization.[4]

The restoration plan in Haggai and First Zechariah (hereafter referred to as 1-Zech.) is of a different sort. The activity of both prophets was during the years 520–519, when the genesis of the post-exilic community had already begun, so this plan was notably more realistic and concrete than those already discussed. A certain realism appears because two actual historical personalities are included in the plan—the Davidide Zerubbabel and the Zadokite Jeshua. In modern biblical analysis there are two views about what the prophets expected; either restoration of the Davidic monarchy[5] or a partnership of the secular and religious powers in a diarchy.[6] The latter appears to be

and in Qumran Literature', *BM*, p. 55.

1. E. Speiser, 'Background and Function of the Biblical Nasi', *OBS*, p. 114.

2. M. Noth, *Das System der zwölf Stämme Israels* (BWANT, 4; Stuttgart, 1930), pp. 151-62; G. Buccellati, *Cities and Nations of Ancient Syria: An Essay on Political Institutions with Special Reference to the Israelite Kingdoms* (Rome, 1967), pp. 122-24.

3. Speiser, 'Background', pp. 116-21.

4. Speiser, 'Background', pp. 121-22; see also T.E. Fretheim, 'The Priestly Document: Anti-Temple?', *VT* 18 (1968), pp. 313-29; R.G. Hamerton-Kelly, 'The Temple and the Origins of Jewish Apocalyptic', *VT* 20 (1970), pp. 4-5.

5. J.W. Rothstein, *Die Nachtgesichte des Sacharja* (BWANT, 8; Leipzig, 1910), pp. 121-39; M. Zer-Kabod, *The Books of Haggai, Zechariah, and Malachi* [Hebrew] (Jerusalem, 1957); and also 'Issues in the Book of Zechariah' [Hebrew], *PHLHB*, II, p. 120.

6. E. Sellin, *Studien zur Entstehungsgeschichte der jüdischen Gemeinde nach dem Exil*, II (Leipzig, 1901), pp. 164-78; J. Liver, *The History of the Davidides: From the Destruction of the State of Judah to the Destruction of the Second Temple* [Hebrew] (Jerusalem, 1959), pp. 75, 95-103; K. Koch, 'Haggais unreines Volk', *ZAW* 79 (1967), pp. 52, 65-66.

the correct view (see Zech. 4.14; 6.13).

With this, one can conclude that in the sixth century BCE there were many different and multifaceted plans for restoration among those not deported from Judah, as well as among the exiles in Babylon—all of whom stroved for a more or less independent political organization in Judah or Palestine, but who envisioned the forms of this organization differently. Which of these plans were carried out, and to what extent? The answer depends on features of the internal development of the postexilic community and its situation in Palestine, its confrontation with the other socio-political structures in Palestine, and the Achaemenid politics in the Palestine area.

III

After the conquest of Babylon, Cyrus II conquered Syria and Palestine as well. The assumption[1] that Persian control was only nominal in the time of Cyrus II has been convincingly refuted,[2] but Alt, Galling, Kreissig, Rainey, and others,[3] rightly claim that within the newly created satrapy, 'Babylon and Across the River', the administrative-territorial division of the Assyrians and Babylonians was maintained. Thus, Judah, which was added to the previously existing Babylonian province of Samaria in the year 582, was counted in the same administrative unit after 539/538.

This situation must be viewed within an understanding of Cyrus's Palestine politics. The major element is the religious and political tolerance that was established, and also the attempt of the Persian king to build in Palestine a secure staging point for the planned conquest of Egypt.[4] This last aim could be achieved through the return of the exiles

1. A. Alt, 'Die Rolle Samarias bei der Entstehung des Judentums', *KSGVI*, II, pp. 330-33; K. Galling, 'Syrien in der Politik der Achämeniden bis 448 v. Chr.', *AO* 36 (1937), pp. 15-27; Galling, *Studien*, pp. 37-42; Kreissig, *Sozialökonomische Situation*, p. 37.

2. Klausner, *History*, I, pp. 186-87; J. Liver, 'The Beginning of the Return' [Hebrew], *E-I* 5 (1958), p. 119; A.F. Rainey, 'The Satrapy *Beyond the River*', *AJBA* 1 (1969), pp. 51-52.

3. Alt, 'Rolle', pp. 333-37; Galling, *Studien*, pp. 47-48; M. Noth, *Die Welt des Alten Testaments* (Berlin, 1957), pp. 80-81; Kreissig, *Sozialökonomische Situation*, p. 39; Rainey, 'Satrapy', pp. 62-63.

4. M.A. Dandamaev, *Iran during the Reign of the First Achaemenids* [Russian] (Moscow, 1963), pp. 110-14; Kreissig, *Situation*, p. 37.

to Judah, and these suggestions led to the publication of the edict of Cyrus II in the year 539/538.

This edict, in both its variants, was the starting point for the return of the exiles. The Aramaic *dikrônâ* (Ezra 6.3-5) was an official memorandum for the Persian administration that controlled the distribution of money, wool and food. The Hebrew version (Ezra 1.2-4) was an oral call to exiles.[1] But was this edict, as many have assumed,[2] also the point of origin for the rebuilding of an administration in Judah? In order to answer this question, both variants must be examined:

	Hebrew Variant (Ezra 1.2-4)	Aramaic Variant (Ezra 6.3-5)
1	Permission for a return to Jerusalem	-
2	Permission to rebuild the temple in Jerusalem	Order to rebuild the temple by help from state treasury
3	Permission for a collection for the returning exiles	-
4	-	Order to return the plundered templewares

Table 1

In neither of the variants is the question regarding the political-administrative organization of Judah mentioned. Such caution on the part of Cyrus II is understandable because the return had only begun and it was impossible to predict its scope and the position of the returnees in Judah. Therefore the Persian central administration avoided any administrative change in Palestine that might have provoked the animosity of the real power in the land, such as the Samarians and Ammonites.

However, the returning exiles, who were not really very numerous at first, could not stand up to the established Palestinian population without support from the central power.[3] The temple of Yahweh became this necessary support for the repatriates. The building of the temple was initiated by the central administration and served as a gathering point as well as a point of solidarity for the *bēt 'ābôt*. The

1. J.P. Weinberg, 'Demographische Notizen zur Geschichte der nachexilischen Gemeinde in Juda', *Klio* 54 (1972), pp. 50-51.

2. For example, L. Rost, 'Erwägungen zum Kyroserlass', *Verbannung und Heimkehr: Beiträge zur Geschichte und Theologie Israels im 6. und 5. Jh v. Chr.* (Tübingen, 1961), pp. 302-303.

3. J.P. Weinberg, 'Der *'am hā'āreṣ* des 6–4 Jh. v.u.Z.', *Klio* 56 (1974), pp. 329-33.

temple was a symbol which revealed the favour of Yahweh and the good-wishes of Cyrus. That is why the leaders of the Samarians complained that the rebuilding of the temple and the city might possibly cause revolt (Ezra 4.9-16). It is hard to determine how valid such an accusation was,[1] but the concerns correspond to the political interests of Cambyses, who intensified the control of the Persian central power over the great temples.[2] The complaint of the Samarians was successful, however, and the temple construction was temporarily halted (Ezra 4.24).

The administrative reorganization of the empire by Darius I led to a separation of Abar-nahara as a special fifth satrapy.[3] At the same time, a new edict regarding the community in Judah was published. The edict of Darius is available in two variants, but the majority of scholars[4] deny the authenticity of the second variant with some justification. 2 Esd. 4.47-57 and *Ant.* 11.3.8 most probably belong to the second century BCE retelling of these events. The authentic first version (Ezra 6.7-12; 1 Esd. 6.27-33) contains the following orders:

1. to continue on with the temple building,
2. to support the temple by the fiscal organization,
3. to supply the temple with offering gifts,
4. death penalty and property confiscation for any violator of the edict.

The content of the edict proves that no significant change in the Achaemenid administration of Palestine was initiated, but the authority of the central power over the temple and emerging community was somewhat strengthened, which doubtless solidified the

1. Although the theory of an uprising led by Zerubabbel, once supported by Sellin (*Studien*, I, pp. 178-97) and others (W.F. Albright, *From the Stone Age to Christianity* [New York, 1957], p. 324; J. Morgenstern, 'Jerusalem—485 BC', *HUCA* 27 [1956], pp. 167-74), has been called into question (Galling, *Studien*, pp. 147-48; J. Liver, 'Zerubbabel', *EB*, II [Hebrew], pp. 938-42), one can hardly doubt the possibility of an active agitation for independence (A.T. Olmstead, *History of Palestine and Syria* [New York, 1931], pp. 556-75; *History of the Persian Empire* [Chicago, 1948], p. 136).

2. Dandamaev, 'Temple', p. 38.

3. Rainey, 'Satrapy', p. 53.

4. A. Bentzen, *Introduction to the Old Testament*, II (Copenhagen, 1957), pp. 219-20; S. Mowinckel, *Studien zu dem Buche Ezra–Nehemia*, I (Oslo, 1964), pp. 7-12.

position of the latter in Palestine. Although the members of the emerging community, as also the remaining general population of Judah, stood under the administration of the province of Samaria and the other provinces, the community already possessed a very limited self-government before 458/457 BCE.

Three figures of the community before 458/456 are known to us—Sheshbazzar,[1] the Davidide Zerubbabel and the Zadokite Jeshua/Jehoshua, who are mentioned without a title, as often as they are mentioned with a title. Table 2 compares all the places where these figures are mentioned, and the number of times that a name appears with or without a title:

	T	Ezra 1–6				Haggai				I-Zechariah			
		a	b	c	d	a	b	c	d	a	b	c	d
Sheshbazzar	4	1	1	-	2	-	-	-	-	-	-	-	-
Zerubbabel	17/18	-	1?*	-	6	-	4	-	3	-	-	-	4
		e	f	g		e	f	g		e	f	g	
Jeshua	17	-	-	5		-	5	-		1	3	3	

T = Total number of times the leader is mentioned.
a = *nāśî* b = *peḥâ* c = *tiršātā* d = without title
e = priest f = high priest g = without title.
* In Ezra 6.7 perhaps a reference to Zerubbabel.

Table 2

Before we analyse the information presented here, we must consider the titles that are mentioned. The Aramaic word *peḥâ* indicates the satrap and the provincial governor, but only in combination with the indication of the area or ethnic group under his command (Ezra 6.13; Neh. 5.14) or with an indication of the responsibility assigned to him.[2]

1. Against the view of Nikel (*Die Wiederherstellung des jüdischen Gemeinwesens nach dem babylonischen Exil* [Freiburg i.B., 1900], pp. 44-52) that identified Sheshbazzar with the Davidide Shenazzar, see P.R. Berger ('Zu der Namen Scheschbazzar und Schinazzar', *ZAW* 83 [1971], pp. 98-100). Although the identification of Sheshbazzar as a Davidide is not impossible (Liver, *History*, pp. 8-11; Galling, *Studien*, pp. 132-34), the view of Brand, identifying Sheshbazzar with Zerubbabel, is hardly credible (J. Brand, 'Notes for an Article on the Second Temple' [Hebrew], *Tarbiz* 29 (1960), pp. 210-11).

2. O. Leuze, *Die Satrapieneinteilung in Syrien und im Zweistromlände von 520 bis 320* (Halle, 1935), p. 18.

According to Galling,[1] *tiršātā* is a formal term of address for a highly placed person; for Mowinckel and Benveniste,[2] it is an Iranian personal name, while de Lagarde, Hinz and Lifschitz[3] suggest that this Aramaic title corresponds to the Iranian term for governor. Bogoljubov[4] translates *tiršātā* as 'the one who assists with eating and drinking', that is 'cup-bearer', which would indicate Nehemiah's function as *tiršātā* (Neh. 1.11, etc.). The titles *hakkōhēn* and *hakkōhēn haggādôl* mean, in reference to Jeshua/Jehoshua, 'high priest'.[5]

If we now refer to the data provided in Table 2, the number of times when a title is not mentioned is striking; with Sheshbazzar, two of 4 (50%), with Zerubbabel 13 of 17/18 (76/72%) and with Jeshua/Jehoshua, 8 of 17 (47%)—which can hardly be accidental in the context of the highly 'title granting' and 'title conscious' Near East. The absolute majority of all names with titles occur in the narrative parts of Ezra 1–6 and mainly in the prophetic narratives of Haggai and Zechariah; with Sheshbazzar, 100%, Zerubbabel, 80% and with Jeshua/Jehoshua, 100%; and they are almost entirely absent (the only exception being Ezra 6.7) in the official documents of the Persian administration. It is possible to explain this by suggesting that these three figures carried no official titles, and the references to titles only express the hopes and struggles of the emergent community.

This would also explain the real function of Sheshbazzar and Zerubbabel. Sheshbazzar, who is given the title *nāśî* and *peḥâ*, was neither governor of Judah nor fully empowered 'commissar' for the temple construction,[6] but only the leader of a group of returnees. The temple supplies were handed over to this official, who then laid the foundation of the temple (Ezra 5.16). Zerubbabel was not a governor

1. Galling, *Studien*, p. 81.

2. E. Benveniste, *Titres et noms propres en iranien ancien* (Paris, 1966), p. 120; Mowinckel, *Studien*, I, pp. 99-109.

3. I express my gratitude to V.D. Lifschitz for this information.

4. M.N. Bogoljubov, 'The Old Persian Name for Cup-Bearer' [Russian], *Problems of Iranian Studies and Indo-European Comparative Linguistics* (Moscow, 1970), p. 40.

5. J. Morgenstern, 'A Chapter in the History of the High Priesthood', *AJSL* 55 (1938), pp. 1-24; J. Gabriel, *Untersuchungen über das alttestamentliche Hohepriestertum* (Vienna, 1933), pp. 1-7.

6. Galling, *Studien*, p. 133; Klausner, *History*, I, pp. 150-53; Liver, *History*, pp. 79-81; Meyer, *Entstehung*, pp. 75-79; Zucker, *Studien*, pp. 19-20.

of Judah,[1] but merely an unofficial leader of the community and the temple construction.

It is interesting to compare this to the frequent mention of the *šābê yᵉhûdāyê*, that is, the elders of the Jews in the official Persian documents. They answer the inquiry of the satrap Tattnai (Ezra 5.5, 9). The edict of Darius I addresses them in order to continue the temple construction (Ezra 6.7, 8, 14). It is not outside the realm of possibility that the *šābê yᵉhûdāyê* was the leading committee, a standing council composed of twelve persons[2] (Neh. 7.7; Ezra 8.24).

Until 458/457, the postexilic community was still not a defined citizen–temple community, but an organism in an emerging status. Correspondingly, the Persian central power avoided all administrative changes and privileges that could promote the development of this emerging community to a particular power. Nevertheless, this amorphous structure carried in itself the seeds of the later citizen–temple community and local power.

IV

In the middle to second half of the fifth century BCE, radical changes took place in the community—the territory it occupied enlarged significantly, and the number of the community members grew. Also, the position of the lay groups—the *bāttê 'ābôt*, and the influence of the priesthood both increased.[3] Such a growth of the community also provoked the opposing power in Palestine,[4] which is possibly associated with the centrifugal opposition movements in the midst of the fifth century BCE in the Achaemenid Empire—mainly in the neighboring areas in Egypt and Syria.[5]

The issuing of the edict of Artaxerxes I (Ezra 7.11-26) is understandable under such circumstances although its meaning and

1. Klausner, *History*, I, pp. 186-87; Liver, *History*, p. 72; Zucker, *Studien*, pp. 19-20.

2. Compare the existence of the elders in pre-exilic time; see D.G. Evans, 'Advisers at Shechem and Political Institutions at Israel and Sumer', *JNES* 25 (1966), pp. 274-76; A. Malamat, 'Kingship and Council in Israel and Sumer', *JNES* 22 (1963), pp. 247-53.

3. Weinberg, 'Notizen', pp. 55-57; 'Das *Bēit 'Āḇōt* im 6–4 Jh. v.u.Z.', *VT* 23 (1973), pp. 411-12.

4. Weinberg, '*'Am hā'āreṣ*', pp. 333-34.

5. Rainey, 'Satrapy', pp. 64-65.

purpose is disputed in the scientific literature. For Rost,[1] the edict is 'the birth of post-biblical Judaism'; Galling[2] sees it as only the authorization of Ezra, while Mowinckel[3] is of the opinion that the edict establishes the economic and legal status of the community in the Achaemenid kingdom. A comparison of the purposes of this edict with those of the edicts of Cyrus and Darius will lead to a clarification of the problem:

	Edict of Artaxerxes I	Edicts of Cyrus	Darius
1	Permission to return, and to collect means for the returnees.	+	-
2	Support of the temple cult by fisc;	-	+
3	Tax exemption for priests, temple singers, gatekeepers, etc.	-	-
4	Establishment of jurisdition and assignment of own judge	-	-
5	Assignment of punishment for anyone who violates	-	-

Table 3

Before I consider the unique features of the edict of Artaxerxes, the question of the authorization of Ezra in the year 458[4] must be answered, because many scholars[5] believe that the work of Ezra was only of a religious nature. Other scholars[6] see Ezra as a Persian official among the exiles, while for Galling[7] Ezra was a special emissary with certain limited powers. As distinct from the untitled Sheshbazzar and Zerubbabel, in the edict of Artaxerxes I, the Zadokite Ezra was indicated mostly by the title *kōhēn* (e.g. Ezra 7.11, 12, 21) and *sōpēr* (e.g. Ezra 7.6, 12, 21). If it is the case that the title *kōhēn* proves the association of Ezra with the priesthood, the title *sōpēr*[8] (which designated an official of the pre-exilic Jewish kingdom as well as the Achaemenid administration), shows that Ezra was an

1. Rost, 'Kyroserlass', pp. 303-304.
2. Galling, *Studien*, pp. 165-78.
3. Mowinckel, *Studien*, III, pp. 20-35.
4. The traditional date for the mission of Ezra has also been supported by recent studies (Weinberg, 'Notizen', p. 52; Rainey, 'Satrapy', pp. 62-63; Dandamaev, *Politische Geschichte*, p. 27; and others).
5. Mowinckel, *Studien*, III, pp. 117-24; C. North, 'Civil Authority in Ezra', *Studi in onore di E. Volterra*, VI (Mailand, 1969), pp. 377-404.
6. H.H. Schaeder, *Esra der Schreiber* (Tübingen, 1930), pp. 39-49; Liver, 'The Time', pp. 18-19; Olmstead, *History*, pp. 304-307.
7. Galling, *Studien*, pp. 178-81.
8. Schaeder, *Esra*, pp. 42-49.

officially installed representative of the central administration who was assigned 'to conduct an investigation about Judah and Jerusalem according to the law of your God' (Ezra 7.14).

What was new in the edict of Artaxerxes is the allowance of a tax-exemption for all the community members,[1] by means of which the citizen–temple community was separated from the surrounding socio-political structure. The latter, in all probability, paid these taxes. Even more significant was the concession of a jurisdiction on the basis of 'the law of the God of heaven' (Ezra 7.23). With this, a decisive step was taken toward the establishment of the community as an independent entity, among whom was already an awareness that 'we are slaves, but our God has not forgotten us in our slavery; he has extended his faithful love to us even under the kings of Persia and revived us to rebuild the temple of God, restore its ruins and provide us with a refuge (*geder*) in Judah and Jerusalem...' (Ezra 9.9). This verse proves that the decisive power in the community distanced itself from the earlier struggle for independence and that the dependence of the community on the Persian central administration was recognized as indisputable. It was acknowledged that thanks only to the help and support of the Achaemenids the community was organized, the temple rebuilt and a *geder* (refuge) given. The word *geder* is frequently used in the Old Testament to refer to God's protection over his people, which brought about the isolation of God's people (e.g. Mic. 7.11; Ezek. 13.5; Ps. 80.13). Ezra 9.9 is also to be read in this sense and indicates that for the community, the most important result of the edict of Artaxerxes was the separation and formation of the citizen–temple community.

However, the edict of Artaxerxes I created a paradox, and therefore at the same time an especially explosive situation in Palestine, because the members of the community's administration were subject to the governors of the provinces, that is, mainly to the *peḥâ* of Samaria.

The first step toward overcoming this paradoxical situation was the establishment of an independent province of 'Yehud' in the middle of the fifth century BCE.[2] Stern[3] has recently provided an important

1. J.P. Weinberg, '*Netînîm* und "Söhne der Sklaven Salomos" im 6.–4. Jh. v.u.Z.', *ZAW* 87 (1975), pp. 365-68.

2. Alt, 'Rolle', pp. 330-33; Kreissig, *Situation*, pp. 107-11.

3. E. Stern, 'Seal-Impression in the Achaemenid Style in the Province of Judah', *BASOR* 202 (1971), pp. 6-16.

argument for the dating of the organization of the province of Yehud. The majority of the approximately 65 unmarked non-inscribed stamps from Achaemenid Judah, as well as the so-called '*yhwd*-stamps', are assigned to the middle of the fifth century BCE, which shows that Judah freed herself from the control of Samaria to become an independent province. However, it must be remembered that the recently formed province of Judah is not to be identified with the citizen–temple community, which consisted of only about 70% of the residents of Judah, at the end of 458/457 BCE, living in the six isolated areas within the province of Yehud.[1] It is more correct and precise to speak about the citizen–temple community in the province of Yehud, because the difference between them was not only geographical or spatial, but lay mostly in the political realm. The province of Yehud was an institution of the central administration, while the citizen–temple community became a local administration.

The activity of Nehemiah played a decisive role in this evolution of the citizen–temple community toward local administration. As *tiršātā*, that is, the courtier nearest the king, Nehemiah requested from Artaxerxes I permission to go to Jerusalem (Neh. 2.5-9). And 'from that day on it fell to me to be their *peḥâ* in the land of Judah' (Neh. 5.14). According to this evidence Nehemiah was officially installed—but with what authority? The key to the solution of the question lies in the peculiar formulation of the office of Nehemiah. The title *peḥâ* is, in Neh. 5.14, not connected with a toponym (cf. *tattᵉnai paḥat 'abar-nahᵃrâ* in Ezra 5.6, and *bagôhî paḥat yᵉhûd* in Cowley 30.1), but is rather assigned with the possessive pronoun, substituting an ethnonym, probably *yᵉhûdîm*[2] (compare *paḥat yᵉhûdāyê* in Ezra 6.7). This allows the supposition that Nehemiah was not *peḥâ* of the province of Yehud, but was rather only *peḥâ* of the community in the land of Judah. There are three other arguments in support of this:

1. All the initiatives of Nehemiah when he was '*peḥâ* of those in the land of Judah', such as the wall construction (Neh. 3), and the synoikism of Jerusalem (Neh. 9), the organization of the home guard (*Landwehr*) and the introduction of the constitution (Neh. 10), involve only the community and not the province of Yehud. When the *'addîrîm* from Tekoa refused to take part in the wall construction (Neh. 3.5),

1. Weinberg, 'Notizen', pp. 54-58.
2. Weinberg, '*'Am hā'āreṣ*', pp. 328-29.

Nehemiah could not pressure them because he was only a leader of the community to which these people did not belong.

2. The conclusion of Meyer[1] that the *pelek* mentioned in Nehemiah 3 was an administrative unit is generally recognized, but it must be more precisely determined whether one is refering to the area of the province of Yehud, or to the citizen–temple community. The studies of Alt, Aharoni, and others[2] prove the stability and continuity of the territorial administrative division of Judah in the eleventh to sixth centuries BCE. Only one of the two overseers of the two halves of the area of Bet-Zur participated in the Jerusalem wall construction, which would hardly be possible if the *pelek* was an administrative unit of the citizen–temple community. One can safely assume that *pelek* indicates a territorial-administrative unity of the province of Jehud, and the *śārîm* were in charge of the Persian provincial administration, and participated in the wall building merely as private persons or as influential members of the citizen–temple community. With regard to these persons, there is also the notice that indicates that 'Shallum, son of Hallohesh, the chief of the half-area Jerusalem, he and his daughters' (Neh. 3.12) built a portion of the wall.

3. In his activity as '*peḥâ* of those in the land of Judah', Nehemiah was supported by the *śārîm*, *ḥōrîm* and *s*[e]*gānîm*. The meaning of these terms is controversial. Bevan[3] doubted the possibility of clarifying the content of the terms; for Meyer, de Vaux, Vogt and others,[4] they are all identical, but according to Zucker, Mowinckel and others[5] these terms indicate different categories of the officers of the Persian province of Yehud. In Table 4, the number of isolated references to these terms in Ezra–Nehemiah is set out, as well as the number of times they are found in different combinations.

1. Meyer, *Entstehung*, p. 166; Klausner, *History*, II, pp. 21-22.

2. A. Alt, 'Judas Gaue unter Josia', *KSGVI*, II, pp. 276-88; 'Bemerkungen zu einigen jüdäischen Ortslisten des Alten Testaments', *KSGVI*, II, pp. 289-305; Y. Aharoni, 'Districts of Israel and Judah' [Hebrew], *BBR*, pp. 110-31; F. Pintore, 'I dodici intendenti di Salomone', *RSO* 45 (1970), pp. 177-207.

3. E.R. Bevan, *Jerusalem under the High Priests* (London, 1930), pp. 5-6.

4. Meyer, *Entstehung*, pp. 132-33; R. de Vaux, *Les institutions de l'Ancien Testament*, I (Paris, 1958), pp. 108-11; F.C.M. Vogt, *Studie zur nachexilischen Gemeinde in Esra–Nehemia*, I (Weil, 1966), pp. 107-108.

5. Zucker, *Studien*, pp. 22-25; Mowinckel, *Studien*, I, pp. 137-39.

Ezra			Nehemiah			
śārîm	*haśśārîm w^{e}hass^{e}gānîm*	*haśśārîm w^{e}hazz^{e}qēnîm*	*śārîm*	*ḥōrîm*	*s^{e}gānîm*	*ḥōrîm w^{e}hass^{e}gānîm*
7	1	1	5	2	4	5

Table 4

The table proves that *śārîm* and *ḥōrîm* are never associated, while both terms are often combined with the conjunction *w-*, with the title *sāgān*. One can assume that the terms *śārîm–ḥōrîm* are semantically close, and their meanings are to be differentiated from the term *s^{e}gānîm* that is combined with either of them.

The validity of this preliminary assumption can be strengthened through analysis of the terms. The term *śar*, which indicated an officer of the civil and military administration in the pre-exilic kingdom,[1] is used in two forms in Ezra–Nehemiah. In construct the state with the words *pelek* (Neh. 3.12), *melek* (Ezra 7.28; 8.25) and others it indicates a representative of the Persian central administration, but much more often, it is used in combination with the words *kōh^{a}nîm* (e.g. Ezra 8.24), *l^{e}wîyîm* (Ezra 8.29) and *'ābôt* (Ezra 8.29). Noting that the word *rō'š*, as the common designation of the head of the *bēt 'ābôt*,[2] disappeared from the linguistic use of the community, so the conclusion seems to be that the *śārîm* of the priests, Levites and *'ābôt* were heads of these agnatic bands in the community.

In the pre-exilic parts of the Old Testament (cf. 1 Kgs 21.8; Jer. 7.20; etc.) *ḥōrîm* is an indication of the notables in the Israelite-Judaean society, while in the Aramaic epigraphy, *ḥôr* is a 'notable', or 'noble'.[3] In Neh. 6.17 the *ḥōrê y^{e}hûdâ* are leaders of those *bāttê 'ābôt* who supported Tobiah. Therefore *ḥōrîm* was not a title of representatives, officials of the central administration, but rather a designation of the heads of the *bāttê 'ābôt* or the influential families within them. The terms *śārîm* and *ḥōrîm* are semantically similar and therefore they are never used in combination with one another in Ezra–Nehemiah.

The term *sgn*, so widely known in the Semitic-speaking Near East,

1. Sh. Yeivin, 'The Administration of Israel' [Hebrew], *BBR*, pp. 47-65.
2. Weinberg, '*Bēit 'Āḇōt*', p. 409; J.R. Bartlett, 'The Use of the Word *Rošh* as a Title in the Old Testament', *VT* 19 (1969), pp. 7-8.
3. J. Liver, '*ḥôrîm*' [Hebrew], *EB*, III, pp. 288-89.

indicates in Ugarit the *maire du palais*;[1] in the pre-exilic sections of the Old Testament it means a highly placed dignitary of the neo-Assyrian and neo-Babylonian kingdom; and in the Elephantine archive it means 'prefect' or 'governor' (e.g. Cowley 10.13). The function of the *s^e^gānîm* is most distinctly expressed in Neh. 13.11, where Nehemiah accused them, but not the *śārîm* or *ḥōrîm*, of not giving the Levites tithe in due. In the last century BCE, the *segen* was a representative of the high priest (*m. Yoma* 3.9; 4.1; *m. Tamid* 7.3),[2] so it is possible that in Ezra–Nehemiah, *s^e^gānîm* were connected with the temple administration. In any case, *śārîm*, *ḥōrîm*, and *s^e^gānîm* were not officers of the central administration, but were representatives of the local administration, that is, functionaries of the self-government of the citizen–temple community in the province of Yehud.

All that has been said thus far confirms the assumption that Nehemiah, as the '*peḥâ* of those in the land of Judah' was not the governor of the province Yehud, but was rather an official leader of the autonomous citizen–temple community, that is, the local government by now established. The community possessed quite an extensive authority that was not purely religious, including the right to fortify Jerusalem and organize a home guard, establish the synoikism, and introduce a constitution with its own jurisdiction which involved only the citizen–temple community. But its authority was strictly separated from the authority of the local representative of the central power of the *paḥat* Yehud.

V

In the last century of the Achaemenid Empire, centrifugal forces gained strength which burst out in almost unstoppable revolts and uprisings. Many of these affected Judah, such as the Tennes Rebellion.[3] Although not determinative, this situation influenced some transformations that took place in the community during the fourth

1. E. Lipiński, 'Recherches ugaritiques 6, Ba'lu-Saduq, maire du palais', *Syria* 56 (1963), pp. 1-2.

2. A. Büchler, *Die Priester und der Cultus im letzten Jahrzehnt des jerusalemischen Temples* (Vienna, 1895) pp. 105-18; R.A. Henshaw, 'The Office of *šaknu* in Neo-Assyrian Times II', *JAOS* 88 (1968), p. 467.

3. D. Barag, 'The Effects of the Tennes Rebellion on Palestine', *BASOR* 183 (1966), pp. 6-12; Kreissig, *Situation*, pp. 7, 112-13.

century BCE. Two of them appear to be particularly important for our problem; the final construction of the leadership of the citizen–temple community and the further evolution of the relationship of the central and local administration in Judah.

For a socio-political organization that is centred on the temple, it is natural and necessary that the high priest of the temple stands at the head. So it was in the citizen–temple communities of Mesopotamia, Asia Minor and Armenia, for example.[1] But what is the position of the Jerusalem high priest in the community of the sixth to fifth centuries BCE? The widely held view[2] that after the decline of Zerubbabel the leadership passed to the Zadokite high priest is not supported from the historical data. The officiating high priest of that time played only a limited role in such decisive activities as the reading of the Torah through Ezra (Neh. 8.1-9, 36), the separation of the mixed marriages (Ezra 10), the wall building (Neh. 3), the introduction of the constitution (Neh. 10), the appointment of lay officials of the temple by Nehemiah (Neh. 13.12), and the revocation of the orders of the high priest Eliashib (Neh. 13.4-8).

However, the place of the high priest in the citizen–temple community at the end of the fifth century BCE is entirely different. In the report of Josephus about the stormy events in the community (*Ant.* 11.7.1-2), the high priest of Jerusalem stands at its head. According to Judith (4.8; 15.8; etc.),[3] the high priest is the leader of the community and in the letter of the leader of the Elephantine community in the year 407 to the governor of Judah, Bagohi, a previous letter is mentioned that was sent to 'our lord, to Yehohanan, the high priest and his colleagues the priests who are in Jerusalem, to Ostanes the brother of Anani, and (to) the nobles of the Jews' (Cowley 30.17-19). It appears that at the turn of the century, the Zadokite high priest is actually the leader of the citizen–temple community.[4]

1. H. Tadmor, *The Temple City and the Royal Cities in Babylon and Assyria* [Hebrew] (Jerusalem, 1967), pp. 182-83; Perichanian, *Temple*, pp. 172-73.

2. Liver, *Time*, pp. 6-7.

3. On the possible dating of the book of Judith in the time of the Achaemenids, cf. G. Brunner, *Der Nabuchodonosor des Buches Judith* (Berlin, 1959); C. Schedl, 'Nabuchodonosor, Arpakšad und Darius', *ZDMG* 115 (1965), pp. 242-45.

4. Compare Morgenstern, *Chapter*, pp. 360-77; F. Stummer, 'Gedanken über die Stellung des Hohenpriesters in der alttestamentichen Gemeinde', *Episcopus*, pp. 24-25.

In Judith (4.8; 15.8; etc.) the *gerousia* that is next to the high priest is mentioned, while in Cowley 30.19, the institution of the *ḥōrê yᵉhûdāyê* is named. The term *yᵉhûdîm-yᵉhûdāyê* was already at this time the dominant self-identification of the community,[1] so the *ḥōrê yᵉhûdāyê* was not an institution of the provincial administration of Yehud, but rather an organ of the self-administration of the citizen–temple community. Although the available evidence does not entirely prove it, the relationship of this institution to the assembly of the 150 *hayyᵉhûdîm wᵉhassᵉgānîm* (Neh. 5.17) or to the later Sanhedrin,[2] allows one to suggest that the gerousia of the people—*ḥōrê yᵉhûdāyê*— was a standing council of notables directly associated with the high priest, perhaps similar to the *puḫru* in the Mesopotamian citizen–temple community.[3]

This fully constructed local administration, that is, the self-governing citizen–temple community, was strictly separated from the central administration of the province of Yehud. Josephus (*Ant.* 11.7.1-2) viewed the intervention of the *peḥâ* Bagoas in the internal affairs of the community as a gross and wilful attack against its autonomy and privileges. The leader of the Elephantine community also sharply differentiated the self-administration of the community from the *paḥat yᵉhûd*, by delivering two letters about one and the same question to the different institutions. It is also striking to note the different use of the toponym *yᵉhûd* and the ethnonym *yᵉhûdāyê* in both letters; while the ethnonym indicated the organ of the self-administration of the community (Cowley 30.19), the toponym is associated with the title *peḥâ* (Cowley 30.1).

Such a co-existence and differentiation between two powers over a small territory was not possible in the long term, especially when the citizen–temple community and the province of Yehud were brought closer to each other both demographically and territorially in the fourth century BCE.[4] This led to the gradual unification of both administrations. We find evidence for this in the numerous epigraphic stamps that can be divided into four types:

1. Weinberg, '*'Am hā'āreṣ*', pp. 328-29.
2. Mowinckel, *Studien*, I, pp. 137-39.
3. J. Klausner, 'The Great Keneset' [Hebrew], *EB*, IV, pp. 193-95; H. Mantel, *Studies in the History of the Sanhedrin* (New York, 1961), pp. 92-101.
4. Weinberg, 'Notizen', p. 58.

1 The non-inscribed stamps
2 The stamps with the inscription *yhwd* (*-yhd, yh*)
3 The stamps with the inscription *yršlm*
4 The stamps with the inscription *mṣh*

Although some scholars[1] assign these stamps to the Hellenistic period, most of them[2] are to be dated in the Achaemenid period. Let us consider the stamp groups.

According to Ginsberg,[3] *mṣh* is an abbreviation of the toponym Mizpah (*Tell en-Nasbe*), but Avigad and Cross[4] identify it with the name of the place Moza in the vicinity of Jerusalem (Jos. 18.26; *m. Sukka* 5.4). Ginsberg and Avigad refer to Neh. 3.7, where the 'men of Gibeon and Mizpah, attached to the throne of the *peḥâ* of Abarnahara (*l*ᵉ*kissē' paḥat 'ēber hannāhār*)' are mentioned as participating in the construction of the wall, from which one can draw the conclusion that Mizpah was 'apparently... a crown land' (Ginzberg) or that Mozah held 'the special status of crown estate' (Avigad).

Stern[5] has convincingly argued that the uninscribed stamps with iconography, 'in a pure Achaemenid style' of the sixth to fifth centuries BCE, which are especially important for our discussion, were in the middle of the fifth century replaced by the *yhwd*-stamps, which stands in connection with the organization of the province of Yehud.

The important *yhwd*-stamps of the late fifth to fourth centuries BCE[6] are extant in four variants:

1 Stamps with the inscription *yhwd* (*-yhd, yh*)
2 Stamps with the inscription *yhwd* + *pḥw'*

1. G. Garbini, 'The Dating of Postexilic Stamps', *ERR*, I, pp. 62-66; P.W. Lapp, 'Ptolemaic Stamped Handles from Judah', *BASOR* 172 (1963), pp. 22-35.

2. W.F. Albright, 'Light on the Jewish State in Persian Times', *BASOR* 53 (1934), pp. 1, 20-22; Y. Aharoni, 'Yehud' [Hebrew], *EB*, III, pp. 484-86; N. Avigad, 'A New Class of Yehud Stamps', *IEJ* 7 (1957), pp. 146-53; 'Yehud or Ha'ir?', *BASOR* 158 (1960), pp. 23-27; F.M. Cross, Jr, 'Judean Stamps', *E-I* 9 (1969), pp. 22-26.

3. H.L. Ginsberg, '*Mmšt* and *Mṣh*', *BASOR* 109 (1948), pp. 21-22.

4. N. Avigad, 'New Light on the MṢH Seal-Impression', *IEJ* 8 (1958), pp. 113-19; Cross, 'Judean Stamps', p. 23.

5. Stern, 'Seal-Impression', pp. 6-16.

6. Cross, 'Judean Stamps', p. 23; J. Naveh, 'The Aramean Imprint of the Yehud Stamps' [Hebrew], *DKHHLH*, pp. 98-100.

3 Stamps with the inscription *yhwd* + personal name and
4 Stamps with the inscription *yhwd* + personal name + *pḥw'*, or personal name + *pḥw'*

The reading *pḥw-paḥwa-peḥâ*, suggested by Aharoni and supported by Kutscher,[1] is disputed by Cross and Naveh[2] but their suggested reading *pḥr'-paḥra* ('potter') is disputable. The word *pḥw'* in combination with *yhwd* proves that the *yhwd* stamps in general were connected with the fiscal policies of the *peḥâ* of the province of Yehud.[3] In the inscriptions *yhwd* + personal name + *pḥw'* or personal + *pḥw'* the following personal names are mentioned: *'Aḥyo*/*'Aḥzai* (*ERR* I, 33–34, No. 2021/I), Ḥanana (*ERR* II, 46, No. 6587/1), Jeho'ezer (*ERR* I, 7-8 No. 161/3) and 'Uriyo.[4] All these names occur in the priestly onomasticon which permits the assumption[5] that in the fourth century BCE the authority of the *peḥâ* of the province of Yehud was transferred to the high priest in Jerusalem.

If Aharoni and Avigad[6] are correct in their claim that in the second half of the fourth century the stamp with the inscription *yršlm* replaced the *yhd* stamp, this change can be explained by the increased role of Jerusalem, and the authorities there, including the increased role of the high priests.

The epigraphic material proves that in the second half of the fourth century BCE the local administration of the province of Yehud was apparently transferred to the head of the citizen–temple community. Two further arguments could be cited in this regard: (1) the coin from Beth-zur with the legend *ḥzkyw*,[7] and (2) the view of Cross: 'It is not improbable that Hezekiah was a high priest during the fourth century',[8] who, as *peḥâ*, also had the authority to mint coins.[9] In the

1. Y. Aharoni, 'Analogues', *ERR*, I, pp. 58-59; Y. Kutscher, '*Pḥw* and its Analogues' [Hebrew], *Tarbiz* 30 (1960), pp. 112-19.

2. Cross, 'Judean Stamps', pp. 24-26; Naveh, 'The Imprint', pp. 99-100.

3. W.F. Albright, 'The Seal from Jericho and the Treasurers of the Second Temple', *BASOR* 148 (1957), pp. 28-30; N. Avigad 'Seal' [Hebrew], *EB*, III, pp. 84-85; Aharoni, 'Yehud', pp. 484-86.

4. P.C. Hammond, *PEQ* 89 (1957), pp. 68-69.

5. Albright, 'Seal', pp. 28-30; Avigad, 'Class', pp. 146; Aharoni, *ERR*, I, pp. 58-59.

6. Aharoni, *ERR*, I, p. 30; Avigad, 'Seal', pp. 84-85.

7. O.R. Sellers, *The Citadel of Beth-Zur* (Philadelphia, 1933), p. 73.

8. Cross, 'Judean Stamps', p. 23.

9. Dandamaev, *Politische Geschichte*, pp. 45-48.

description of the events of the year 332, Josephus mentions only the high priest of Jerusalem (*Ant.* 11.8).

Two related processes took place in the Palestinian citizen–temple community in the fourth century BCE: the full construction of the local administration led by the high priest and the *gerousia*, and the transfer of the function of the *peḥâ* of the province Yehud, that is, the representation of the central administration, to the high priest. It is apparant that the full merger of both powers was not accomplished in the Achaemenid period. It seems more probable that a kind of personal unity was built, in which the previously separated power and function of the local and central power in Judah was unified in the person of the high priest.

The following conclusions can be drawn:

1. The development of the citizen–temple community toward a local administration within the Achaemenid empire was, because of the nature of the community, almost inevitable, but was modified and influenced by other factors—such as the internal development of the community, its setting in the specific territory, the politics of the central administration, and so forth.

2. The assignment by the central administration of the citizen–temple community as the locally organized administration was, in general, benevolent (and it was not seriously damaged by contemporary and local differences) because the Achaemenid considered (justifiably) this form of local administration as more loyal than the other forms (polis, kingdoms, tribes, for example).

3. Such a benevolent assignment, together with the internal evolution of the citizen–temple community, led to the unification, perhaps in the form of a personal union, of the local and central power in the person of the high priest.

Chapter 8

THE POSTEXILIC CITIZEN–TEMPLE COMMUNITY: THEORY AND REALITY

The concept of the postexilic citizen–temple community was elaborated and published in a series of articles (part of which are included in this volume) about twenty years ago. This concept found some support in scientific circles,[1] but objections were also raised, the essence of which were expressed by Kreissig, who wrote: 'The citizen–temple community is only a theory, not a proven one and in my opinion not even a historically necessary structure of the Judaean society in the Achaemenid period'.[2] This objection includes two important and interesting aspects. The first and the wider one concerns the problem of the relation between theory and reality in historical science, while the second and narrower one deals with the question of whether the concept of the citizen–temple community corresponds to the nature of the postexilic Jerusalem community or not. Twenty years is quite a

1. P. Briant, 'Rois, tributs et paysans: Etudes sur les formations tributaires du moyen-orient ancien' (Centre de Recherches d'Histoire Ancienne, 43; Paris, 1982), pp. 291-330; D.L. Smith, *The Religion of the Landless*: *A Sociology of the Babylonian Exile* (Bloomington, 1989), pp. 108ff.; R.P. Carroll, 'Silence, Exile, and Cunning: Reflections on the "Bürger-Tempel-Gemeinde" Thesis Approach to the Early Second Temple Period' (SBL 1990 International Meeting Abstracts; Vienna, 1990), p. 36; H.C. Washington, 'Proverbs and Post-Exilic Society' (SBL International Meeting Abstracts; Rome, 1991), pp. 63-64; P.D. Dion, 'The Civic-and-Temple Community of Persian Period Judea: Neglected Insights from Eastern Europe', *JNES* 50 (1991), pp. 281-87.

2. H. Kreissig, 'Eine beachtenswerte Theorie zur Organisation alt vorderorientalischer Templegemeinden im Achämenidenreich: Zu J.P. Weinberg's "Bürger-Tempel-Gemeinde" in Juda', *Klio* 66 (1984), pp. 35-39; cf. H. Utzschneider, *Das Heiligtum und das Gesetz: Studien zur Bedeutung der sinaitischen Heiligtumstexte (Exod. 25–40; Lev. 3–9)* (OBO, 77; Göttingen, 1988), pp. 292-96.

long time in our swiftly changing world, and in the rapidly developing field of Old Testament studies, with new archaeological and epigraphic data, and especially new ideas, the question of whether the concept of the citizen–temple community is out of date becomes inevitable. To answer this a reconsideration of what was written twenty years ago seems necessary. In connection with this task some theses are also formulated for further discussion.

1. The investigation of the 'obscure period' in ancient Jewish history (sixth to fourth centuries BCE) is hampered by the insufficiency of the available sources and by the many gaps in these sources. All the extant sources can be classified into three different text-groups (including biblical and extrabiblical, archaeological, epigraphical and other materials) which would appear as follows: (1) texts belonging to the Babylonian–Persian period and containing information about Jewish history in this period, (2) texts belonging to the Babylonian–Persian period, but giving information about other, earlier periods of Jewish history and (3), texts of later times, but containing information about the period under discussion. A survey of this material leads to the conclusion that the 'obscure period' is not as obscure as assumed and that it is provided with sources similar in scope to all Near Eastern history as well as other periods of ancient Jewish history. There are gaps of course, such as the time between the completion of the building of the temple 515 BCE and the arrival of Ezra around 458/457 BCE, but it can be supposed that this silence of texts is a silence of history. Those decades are not reflected in texts, because there was nothing worthy of reflection. At times the silence of sources can be very eloquent, the lack of information very informative.[1]

2. The postexilic Jerusalem community must be located not only in the vertical diachronic axis of Jewish history, but also in the horizontal, synchronic context of the *Achsenzeit*, as well as in its Near Eastern version, the so-called 'Near East pre-Hellenism'.[2] The important features of this time are a noticeable intensification and diversification; individualization and democratization of economic activity; an intensive process of urbanization together with the formation of a specific urban psychology, characterized by a physical and psychic mobility; a sceptical attitude toward tradition and predisposition to innovations;

1. J.P. Weinberg, 'Der Chronist und seine Mitwelt' (to be published).

2. J.P. Weinberg, 'Bemerkungen zum Problem "Der Vorhellenismus im Vorderen Orient" ', *Klio* 58 (1976), pp. 5-20.

an overcoming of particularistic closedness and a strengthening of universalistic openness; an active and wide-ranging migration, in the main voluntary, which embraced larger masses of people and wide territories and stimulated the rapprochement and interaction of different cultures; a noticeable complication of the social structure in connection with an appearance of many marginal social groups; an intensive process of individualization and autonomization of humanity together with a dissemination, even revival, of large agnatic and/or territorial units; a formation of vast empires accompanied by the inevitable emergence and dissemination of autonomous, self-governing cities, whose one form was the citizen–temple community in places such as Mesopotamia, Syria, Asia Minor, Armenia; and finally there was the formation of an autonomous intelligentsia, to some degree independent from temple and state, which was the main agent of the gradual transition from the mythological kind of thinking to the scientific-rational one. The main feature of this *Achsenzeit*, 'Near Eastern pre-Hellenism', was the historical context of the Jerusalem community which significantly influenced its nature, although its origin and specificity were determined by the disaster of 586 BCE, the exile, and the events that followed.

3. According to Talmon, Smith and others[1] the disaster of 586 BCE and the exile caused a radical turn in the fate of the Jewish people by abolishing two essential conditions of its existence, namely its monocentrism and relative homogeneity, and by substituting them with a polycentrism and heterogeneity as the result of an enforced dispersed existence in different lands and diverse conditions. The main centres of Jewish existence after 586 BCE and during the exile were Egypt, Mesopotamia and Babylonian Judaea. All centres had many essential features in common, but each of them had peculiarities, especially the Jewish exiles in Mesopotamia and the Jewish population in Babylonian Judaea, who played an important, even decisive role in the formation of the postexilic community.

Common to both Jewish centres, and for the whole nation after BCE, was the total liquidation of the Jewish state and the forcible

1. Sh. Talmon, 'The Emergence of Jewish Sectarianism in the Early Second Temple Period—an Addendum to Max Weber's *Das Antike Judentum*', *The King, Cult and Calendar of Ancient Israel* (Jerusalem, 1986), pp. 176ff.; D.L. Smith, *The Religion of the Landless*, pp. 19ff.; P.R. Ackroyd, *The Chronicler in his Age* (JSOTSup, 101; Sheffield, 1991), pp. 8ff.

depolitization of the whole nation. But this common calamity was experienced and perceived differently in Judaea and Mesopotamia. The Jews who stayed in the conquered Judaea were always reminded of their robbed freedom and independence. They experienced their compulsory transition from the former status of free, fully enfranchised citizens in their own state, into the humiliating status of second-rate, dependent inhabitants in a land no longer their own, much more painfully and tragically (see Lam. 1.1; etc.) than those who were deported. Although the exiled underwent the same degrading change of their social status, it was psychologically easier for them to submit themselves to new conditions (Jeremiah 29) because in Mesopotamia representatives of other ethnic groups, including many Babylonians, belonged to the same social group.

Another consequence of the catastrophe of 586 BCE and the exile was the fundamental change in the structure of Jewish society. In Babylonian Judaea under the influence of the agrarian-social arrangements of the conquerors (2 Kgs 25.12; Jer. 38.10),[1] a simplification and unification of the social structure of the Jewish population took place, in connection with a parallel process of the reinforcement of local territorial communities as necessary substitutes for the destroyed agnatic institutions. For the exiles in Mesopotamia, a conscious consolidation was a *conditio sine qua non* not only of their existence, but also of the preservation of their national identity. In the concrete situation of the exile, the only possible institution fit for this task would be an agnatic community, the *bêt 'ābôt*.

In both centres of Jewish existence the exile was a time of strained, even overstrained, hopes and expectations, which enhanced the development of different plans of restoration. Among the Jews in Babylonian Judaea the hope for a renewal of the previous status quo dominated—the return of the exiles, regaining the land, the rebuilding of the temple and the restoration of the Davidic kingdom. This reflects a distinct orientation of continuity.[2] On the contrary, the 'restoration plan' in the book of Ezekiel (chs. 40–48), which expressed the hopes

1. J.P. Weinberg, 'Die Agrarverhältnisse in der Bürger-Temple-Gemeinde der Achämenidenzeit' *AAASH* 12 (1974), pp. 1-4, 475-81.

2. E. Janssen, *Juda in der Exilszeit: Ein Beitrag zur Frage der Entstehung des Judentums* (FRLANT, 51/69; Göttingen, 1956), pp. 76ff.; J.P. Weinberg, 'Zentral- und Partikulargewalt im achämenidischen Reich', *Klio* 59 (1977), pp. 27-28; D.L. Smith, *The Religion of the Landless*, pp. 34ff.

and intentions of the exiles and maybe the first returnees,[1] is marked by a distinct orientation of discontinuity. It aimed for remarkable innovations, such as the strict separation of the secular/political and social/cultic spheres, radical changes in the position and functions of the head of the state (called the *nāśi* and so forth). Subjective factors, such as the will and intentions of people to establish a state and their enthusiasm about such anticipated developments always plays a formidable role in the genesis of a state, but it can be especially decisive in a case of starting over again, when the restoration of a lost, destroyed state is sought. Therefore the different restoration plans must be taken into account when discussing the origin and development of the postexilic Jerusalem community.

4. The origin and development of this community was determined by three different powers which are to be distinguished in their essence and intentions—the Persian empire, the Jewish exiles in Mesopotamia and the Jewish population in Babylonian Judaea. The participation of the central administration of the Persian empire in the process was determined by the political and strategic interest and needs of the empire and by its preparations for the conquest of Egypt, which called for faithful support in Palestine. These preparations, therefore, could include the foundation of a community of Jewish returnees from Mesopotamia, initiated and supported by the Persian king and therefore grateful and loyal to him. These political–strategic considerations determined the proclamation and the content of the edict of Cyrus II (Ezra 1.3-5), which demonstrates that the Persian central administration considered this formation to be unified by common religious–ideological, economical, social and other interests, but without any distinct political, stately authority and function.[2]

The same edict of Cyrus II states, 'Who is among you of all his people, may his God be with him, let him go up to Jerusalem. . . '

1. H. Gese, *Der Verfassungsentwurf des Ezekiel (Kap. 40–48) traditionsgeschichtlich untersucht* (BHT, 25; Tübingen, 1957), pp. 6ff.; W. Zimmerli, 'Planungen für den Wiederaufbau nach der Katastrophe von 587', *VT* 18 (1968), pp. 229-55; G.Ch. Macholz, 'Noch einmal: Planungen für den Wiederaufbau nach der Katastrophe von 587: Erwägungen zum Schlussteil des sog. "Verfassungsentwurf des Hesekiel" ', *VT* 19 (1969), pp. 322-52; J.P. Weinberg, 'Zentral- und Partikulargewalt im achämenidischen Reich', pp. 29-30; D.L. Smith, *The Religion of the Landless*, pp. 154ff.

2. J.P. Weinberg, 'Zentral- und Partikulargewalt', pp. 29-30; Ackroyd, *Chronicler*, pp. 8ff.

(Ezra 1.3) which indicates that the repatriation of the exiled Jews was not planned, organized or ordered by a Persian administrative measure, but was a wholly voluntary act, dependent only on the free decisions of individuals and groups involved. This fundamental principle of voluntary choice whether to remain in the diaspora or to return to Jerusalem was one of the shaping factors in the emergent community, especially as voluntariness also determined the actions of the third participant in the formation of the Jerusalem community.[1]

The third group consisted of those of the Jewish population in former Babylonian Judaea, who joined the returnees and thus entered the emergent community and were enlisted in the list of its members before 458–456 BCE in Neh. 7/Ezra 2.[2] In this list the people under discussion formed a separate group, and are mentioned in the second place after the returnees. They differ from all other community-members by the details of their identification. In contrast to the returnees, laity, priests, Levites and others, who all were identified according to the formula 'the sons of X' (X is the name of an agnatic formation, of a *bêt 'ābôt*), the group under discussion is mainly identified according to the formula 'the men of A' (A is a toponym), which justifies the proposed designation of this group as 'collectives named by toponyms' and the supposition that this group consisted chiefly of those organized in local, territorial units that represent the Jewish population of northern Judaea.[3]

5. The available demographic data lead to the conclusion that before the year 458/457 BCE, which was a turning-point in the development of the postexilic community, the community included 42,360 members (Neh. 7.66/Ezra 2.64), approximately 13–15% of all the population of Judaea at that time. The settlement of the community did not form a compact territory, but consisted of three spatially isolated enclaves in the coastal area, in the environment of Jerusalem and in the south of the Jordan valley. Although after 458/457 BCE the number of community members increased to 150,000 including approximately

1. J.P. Weinberg, 'Demographische Notizen zur Geschichte der nachexilischen Gemeinde in Juda', *Klio* 54 (1972), pp. 51-53; J.P. Weinberg, 'Zentral- und Partikulargewalt', pp. 30-31; Ackroyd, *Chronicler*, p. 17.

2. J.P. Weinberg, 'Demographische Notizen'.

3. J.P. Weinberg, 'Collectives, Named by Toponyms in Achaemenid Judea' [Russian], *ArOr* 42 (1974), pp. 321-53; S. Japhet, 'People and Land in the Restoration Period', in *Das Land in biblischer Zeit* (Göttingen, 1983), pp. 104-105.

50–60% of the population of Judaea and new territories that were settled in the Shephelah, in the south of Judaea and in the Negev, a caveat must be expressed against the widespread identification of the two terms 'Judaea' and 'postexilic community'. It seems more correct to speak about the postexilic community *in* Judaea (until the middle of the fifth century BCE) and later in the province of Yehud.[1]

6. An essential feature of the postexilic community is its peculiar social structure, including the particular system of agrarian relations, according to which all the land of the community was proclaimed property of God, but was *de facto* the inalienable property of the *bêt 'ābôt* which was divided into parcels for use by the separate families belonging to the *bêt 'ābôt*.[2] Such a system stimulated the social homogeneity of the community, which was manifested in other features of its social organization.

The limited number of slaves (according to Neh. 7.67/Ezra 2.65 only 18% of the number of community members), and the rare and episodic mention of the *tôšāb, śākîr* and especially the *gēr* in the corresponding texts, lead to the conclusion that the postexilic community was essentially an association of free and fully enfranchised people; a uniform, even egalitarian formation. But homogeneity, even equality in estate structure, does not exclude differentiation and stratification on economic, professional and other grounds. Not only the events described in Nehemiah 5, but also the social terminology of that period suggest that such a differentiation and stratification was unknown to the Jerusalem community, especially between the laity and the clergy, and between the priests and the Levites. The data permit us to conclude that before 458/457 BCE the ratio of laity to clergy in the Jerusalem community was 5.4:1, but later changed to 0.8:1, while at the same time the share of the Levites in the clergy increased from 8% to 27%.[3] Such a remarkable growth of the number, and with it the influence, of the clergy made the establishment of a theocratic regime

1. J.P. Weinberg, 'Demographische Notizen', pp. 52-54.

2. J.P. Weinberg, 'Agrarverhältnisse', pp. 481-84.

3. J.P. Weinberg, 'Der *'am hā'āreṣ* des 6.–4. Jh. v.u.Z.', *Klio* 56 (1974), pp. 325-35; 'Slaves and Other Categories of Dependent People in the Palestinian Citizen-Temple-Community of the 6th–4th Centuries BCE' [Russian], *PS* 25 (88) (1974), pp. 63-66; 'Netinim und "Söhne der Sklaven Salomos" im 6.–4. Jh. v.u.Z.', *ZAW* 87 (1975), pp. 355-71; 'Die soziale Gruppe im Weltbild des Chronisten', *ZAW* 98 (1986), pp. 72-95.

possible, but this possibility was not realized mainly because of the balance of power between the three chief 'pillars' of the community—the *bêt 'ābôt*, the town and the Jerusalem temple.

The postexilic *bêt 'ābôt*[1] was an agnatic association, which united real or fictitious families, had a large number of members and a complicated inner structure. It necessarily included genealogies and internal solidarity. The *bêt 'ābôt* was the result of a consciously intended convergence of the former agnatic units that were dissolved during the exile and the early postexilic times such as the *mišpāḥâ*. The *bêt 'ābôt*, whose main function was social, was a form of organization that included not only laymen in the community, but the priests and Levites as well.

The other main form of organization for the community members was the town,[2] especially as the centre of economic activities. The town in the Jerusalem community was self-administered by the elders and judges, but in extraordinary situations a meeting of all the free inhabitants of the town could be summoned. Thus urban self-administration disposed of administrative and juridical matters and perhaps also had some fiscal power on behalf of the *bêt 'ābôt* living in the town and its environment. In postexilic times, Jerusalem was no longer the royal city, but as it was the largest and best-fortified city, the seat of self-government for the community and the town of the temple, it maintained a leading role in the community. But this dominant position of Jerusalem did not turn her into a classical polis. A polis involves a complete fusion of the central town with the *chora*, that is, all the free inhabitants of the town and the free population of the *chora*. During the sixth to fourth centuries BCE Jerusalem did not substitute the community and the community did not become an appendix to Jerusalem.

The 1991 International Meeting of the Society of Biblical Literature in Rome featured a particular interest in the subject of 'The Second Jerusalem Temple'[3] which correlates with the role and significance of

1. J.P. Weinberg, 'Das *Bēit 'Ābōt* im 6.–4. Jh. v.u.Z.', *VT* 23 (1973), pp. 400-14; S. Ben-Dor, *The Bet-Ab in Israel from the Settlement to the End of the Monarchy: The Social Structure of Ancient Israel* [Hebrew] (Haifa, 1986), pp. 111ff.

2. J.P. Weinberg, *The Town in the Palestinian Citizen-Temple-Community of the 6th–4th centuries* BCE (Yerevan, 1973), pp. 149-61.

3. R.P. Carroll, 'So What do we Know about the Temple? The Temple in the Prophets'; P. Marinkovic, 'Was wissen wir über den zweiten Tempel aus Sacharja?',

this institution in the organization and existence of the postexilic community. In the situation of a gradual and protracted voluntary consolidation, the *bêt 'ābôt* of the returnees and the 'collectives named by toponyms', the temple (built by official permission of the Persian central administration) was the main collecting and unifying epicentre of the emergent community, and was an obvious demonstration of the benevolence of the Persian king and a revelation of divine charity.

The *bêt 'ābôt*, the town and the temple were three typologically and functionally different institutions, but they did not form a vertical hierarchic structure with strict order of supremacy and subordination, but were rather a loose horizontal combination of interacting and counterbalancing institutions.

7. It is evident that the postexilic Jerusalem community had some autonomy and self-administration, but the predominating scholarly opinion about a convergence of two essentially different entities—Judaea and the postexilic community—remains the main obstacle for an elucidation of the development, function and authority of this self-administration. Nearly sixty years ago, A. Alt,[1] to his lasting credit, expressed the notion that after the disaster of 586 BCE, Judaea was administratively joined to the existing province of Samerina (Samaria), and that this administrative order prevailed in the Persian era until the time of Nehemiah, when Judaea became a separate province with its own *peḥâ*. In recent work, especially after the publication of the postexilic epigraphical material by Avigad[2] the opinion is often expressed that 'Alt's case. . . collapses',[3] but such a verdict is premature.

Not one of the official documents of the Persian kings, including the edict of Cyrus II and the decree of Darius I (Ezra 6.7-12), contains any hint about an administrative organization of Judaea and the emergent community. It cannot be considered a mere coincidence that in the ancient Near East, which is noted for attention to official titles and

pp. 1-8; D.J.A. Clines, 'Constructing and Deconstructing Haggai's Temple' (SBL, 1991 International Meeting Abstracts), pp. 36-37.

1. A. Alt, 'Die Rolle Samarias bei der Entstehung des Judentums', *KSGVI*, II, pp. 316-37.

2. N. Avigad, *Bullae and Seals from a Post-Exilic Judean Archive* (Qedem Monographs of the Institute of Archaeology; Jerusalem, 1976), pp. 3ff.

3. H.G.M. Williamson, 'The Governors of Judah under the Persians', *TynBul* 39 (1988), p. 77.

status, the leading personalities of the emergent community—Sheshbazzar and Zerubabel—were mentioned mainly without titles in the years 538–515 BCE in *official* documents of the Persian central administration. In the prophecies of Haggai and Zechariah, and in the narrative parts of the book of Ezra, they are mentioned with titles, but this is clearly a demonstration of the wishes and hopes of the returnees in regard to the status of their leaders, rather than a manifestation or confirmation of their officially established and acknowledged status and position. Evidently the emerging postexilic community before 458/457 BCE possessed some very limited self-administration executed by 'the elders of the Jews' (Ezra 5.5-9), but on the whole the community, as well as Judaea, remained subject to the officially installed and acknowledged administration of the province of Samaria.

Changes began in 458/457 BCE, when the edict of Artaxerxes (Ezra 7.11-26) granted the members of the postexilic community tax exemption, their own jurisdiction and other privileges. This was a step toward an official establishment and recognition of the postexilic community as a separate socio-political unit with its own self-administration. The next step in this direction was the foundation of a separate province of Yehud in the middle of the fifth century BCE and the official appointment of Nehemiah as 'the *peḥâ* of those in the land of Judaea' (Neh. 5.14). The unusual formulation of the appointment of Nehemiah permits the supposition that he was *not* made *peḥâ* of the province of Yehud, that is, as a head of the local, provincial branch of the Persian central administration, but only head of the self-administration of the postexilic community *in* the province of Yehud, whose *peḥâ* was another person, maybe Petahiah, the son of Meshezabel 'next to the hand of the [Persian] king in all matters of the people' (Neh. 11.24). This is particularly clear when one notes that all the actions and arrangements of Nehemiah—for example, the reconstruction of the walls of Jerusalem and the synoikism, the solution of the social conflict, the organization of the home guard and the conclusion of the *'ᵃmānâ*—concerned only the community *in* Yehud and not the province of Yehud.

The data provided by Josephus (*Ant.* 11.7.2) and in the book of Judith (e.g. 4.8), the references in the letters of the Elephantine community (Cowley 30.18), the epigraphical and numismatic material, all allow the supposition that at the end of the fifth century and the beginning of the fourth century BCE, the high priests of the Jerusalem temple, the Zadokites, became heads of the self-administration of the community. But this development did not lead to the establishment of a theocracy because of the parity and balance between the three 'pillars' of the community. Neither did it abolish the separation and distinction between the local branch of the Persian central administration and the self-administration of the community.[1]

8. As to the exact delineation of the postexilic community in modern studies, two main approaches can be distinguished. The first one tries to avoid any precise and exact designations or definitions, and contents itself with such neutral terms as 'the postexilic community', 'the Judaean community' and 'the Jerusalem community', whereas the second approach seeks to elaborate as precise and exact as possible designations and definitions which express the nature of this community. The neutrality of the first approach proves in reality to be illusory, so the second approach seems preferable. In the framework of a more precise definition, the proposed designation 'citizen–temple community' seems to be a useful one.

By no means is this designation the only possible and correct one, but some arguments in its favour should be mentioned. The proposed designation puts the postexilic Jerusalem community into one common typological line with other analogous organizations of the *Achsenzeit*, ' Near Eastern pre-Hellenism'—and permits a comparative synchronistic study. This appellation accentuates the dichotomy 'continuity–discontinuity' on the diachronic vertical axis of Jewish history and fixes the essential differences as well as the common features between this organization and those preceding and following it. The designation 'citizen–temple community' correspondingly expresses the nature of this community, because the organization consisted mainly of free, fully-enfranchised members, and because the temple was its collecting and unifying centre, as well as the all-embracing framework for it, and finally because it was a community, that is a consciously and voluntarily formed association.

One concluding remark is that the difference between theory and

1. J.P. Weinberg, 'Zentral- und Partikulargewalt', pp. 25-43; S. Japhet, 'Sheshbazzer and Zerubbabel—Against the Background of the Historical and Religious Tendencies of Ezra–Nehemiah', *ZAW* 94 (1982), pp. 66-98 and *ZAW* 94 (1982), pp. 218-30; E. Stern, 'The Persian Empire and the Political and Social History of Palestine in the Persian Period', in *The Cambridge History of Judaism*, I (Cambridge, 1984), pp. 70-87; H.G.M. Williamson, 'Governors', pp. 59-82.

reality in most spheres of human activity, including historical science, is not so great and fundamental as sometimes imagined, and therefore it seems justified to speak about 'theory and reality' when considering the nature of the Jerusalem citizen–temple community of the sixth to fourth centuries BCE.

INDEXES

INDEX OF REFERENCES

OLD TESTAMENT

Index of Authors

JOURNAL FOR THE STUDY OF THE OLD TESTAMENT

Supplement Series

1 I, HE, WE AND THEY:
A LITERARY APPROACH TO ISAIAH 53
D.J.A. Clines
4 THANKSGIVING FOR A LIBERATED PROPHET:
AN INTERPRETATION OF ISAIAH CHAPTER 53
R.N. Whybray
5 REDATING THE EXODUS AND CONQUEST
J.J. Bimson
6 THE STORY OF KING DAVID:
GENRE AND INTERPRETATION
D.M. Gunn
7 THE SENSE OF BIBLICAL NARRATIVE I:
STRUCTURAL ANALYSES IN THE HEBREW BIBLE (2nd edition)
D. Jobling
10 THE THEME OF THE PENTATEUCH
David J.A. Clines
13 ISAIAH AND THE DELIVERANCE OF JERUSALEM:
A STUDY OF THE INTERPRETATION OF PROPHECY
IN THE OLD TESTAMENT
R.E. Clements
14 THE FATE OF KING SAUL:
AN INTERPRETATION OF A BIBLICAL STORY
D.M. Gunn
15 THE DEUTERONOMISTIC HISTORY
Martin Noth
16 PROPHECY AND ETHICS:
ISAIAH AND THE ETHICAL TRADITION OF ISRAEL
Eryl W. Davies
17 THE ROLES OF ISRAEL'S PROPHETS
David L. Petersen
18 THE DOUBLE REDACTION OF THE DEUTERONOMISTIC HISTORY
Richard D. Nelson
19 ART AND MEANING:
RHETORIC IN BIBLICAL LITERATURE
Edited by David J.A. Clines, David M. Gunn & Alan J. Hauser
20 THE PSALMS OF THE SONS OF KORAH
Michael D. Goulder
21 COLOUR TERMS IN THE OLD TESTAMENT
Athalya Brenner

22 AT THE MOUNTAIN OF GOD:
STORY AND THEOLOGY IN EXODUS 32–34
R.W.L. Moberly

23 THE GLORY OF ISRAEL:
THE THEOLOGY AND PROVENIENCE OF THE ISAIAH TARGUM
Bruce D. Chilton

24 MIDIAN, MOAB AND EDOM:
THE HISTORY AND ARCHAEOLOGY OF LATE BRONZE AND IRON AGE JORDAN AND NORTH-WEST ARABIA
Edited by John F.A. Sawyer & David J.A. Clines

25 THE DAMASCUS COVENANT:
AN INTERPRETATION OF THE 'DAMASCUS DOCUMENT'
Philip R. Davies

26 CLASSICAL HEBREW POETRY:
A GUIDE TO ITS TECHNIQUES
Wilfred G.E. Watson

27 PSALMODY AND PROPHECY
W.H. Bellinger, Jr

28 HOSEA:
AN ISRAELITE PROPHET IN JUDEAN PERSPECTIVE
Grace I. Emmerson

29 EXEGESIS AT QUMRAN:
4QFLORILEGIUM IN ITS JEWISH CONTEXT
George J. Brooke

30 THE ESTHER SCROLL:
THE STORY OF THE STORY
David J.A. Clines

31 IN THE SHELTER OF ELYON:
ESSAYS IN HONOR OF G.W. AHLSTRÖM
Edited by W. Boyd Barrick & John R. Spencer

32 THE PROPHETIC PERSONA:
JEREMIAH AND THE LANGUAGE OF THE SELF
Timothy Polk

33 LAW AND THEOLOGY IN DEUTERONOMY
J.G. McConville

34 THE TEMPLE SCROLL:
AN INTRODUCTION, TRANSLATION & COMMENTARY
Johann Maier

35 SAGA, LEGEND, TALE, NOVELLA, FABLE:
NARRATIVE FORMS IN OLD TESTAMENT LITERATURE
Edited by George W. Coats

36 THE SONG OF FOURTEEN SONGS
Michael D. Goulder

37 UNDERSTANDING THE WORD:
ESSAYS IN HONOR OF BERNHARD W. ANDERSON
Edited by James T. Butler, Edgar W. Conrad & Ben C. Ollenburger

38 SLEEP, DIVINE AND HUMAN, IN THE OLD TESTAMENT
Thomas H. McAlpine

39 THE SENSE OF BIBLICAL NARRATIVE II:
STRUCTURAL ANALYSES IN THE HEBREW BIBLE
David Jobling

40 DIRECTIONS IN BIBLICAL HEBREW POETRY
Edited by Elaine R. Follis

41 ZION, THE CITY OF THE GREAT KING:
A THEOLOGICAL SYMBOL OF THE JERUSALEM CULT
Ben C. Ollenburger

42 A WORD IN SEASON:
ESSAYS IN HONOUR OF WILLIAM MCKANE
Edited by James D. Martin & Philip R. Davies

43 THE CULT OF MOLEK:
A REASSESSMENT
G.C. Heider

44 THE IDENTITY OF THE INDIVIDUAL IN THE PSALMS
Steven J.L. Croft

45 THE CONFESSIONS OF JEREMIAH IN CONTEXT:
SCENES OF PROPHETIC DRAMA
A.R. Diamond

46 THE BOOK OF JUDGES:
AN INTEGRATED READING
Barry G. Webb

47 THE GREEK TEXT OF JEREMIAH:
A REVISED HYPOTHESIS
Sven Soderlund

48 TEXT AND CONTEXT:
OLD TESTAMENT AND SEMITIC STUDIES FOR F.C. FENSHAM
Edited by W. Claassen

49 THEOPHORIC PERSONAL NAMES IN ANCIENT HEBREW:
A COMPARATIVE STUDY
Jeaneane D. Fowler

50 THE CHRONICLER'S HISTORY
Martin Noth
Translated by H.G.M. Williamson with an Introduction

51 DIVINE INITIATIVE AND HUMAN RESPONSE IN EZEKIEL
Paul Joyce

52 THE CONFLICT OF FAITH AND EXPERIENCE IN THE PSALMS:
A FORM-CRITICAL AND THEOLOGICAL STUDY
Craig C. Broyles

53 THE MAKING OF THE PENTATEUCH:
A METHODOLOGICAL STUDY
R.N. Whybray
54 FROM REPENTANCE TO REDEMPTION:
JEREMIAH'S THOUGHT IN TRANSITION
Jeremiah Unterman
55 THE ORIGIN TRADITION OF ANCIENT ISRAEL:
1. THE LITERARY FORMATION OF GENESIS AND EXODUS 1–23
T.L. Thompson
56 THE PURIFICATION OFFERING IN THE PRIESTLY LITERATURE:
ITS MEANING AND FUNCTION
N. Kiuchi
57 MOSES:
HEROIC MAN, MAN OF GOD
George W. Coats
58 THE LISTENING HEART:
ESSAYS IN WISDOM AND THE PSALMS
IN HONOR OF ROLAND E. MURPHY, O. CARM.
Edited by Kenneth G. Hoglund, Elizabeth F. Huwiler, Jonathan T. Glass and Roger W. Lee
59 CREATIVE BIBLICAL EXEGESIS:
CHRISTIAN AND JEWISH HERMENEUTICS THROUGH THE CENTURIES
Edited by Benjamin Uffenheimer & Henning Graf Reventlow
60 HER PRICE IS BEYOND RUBIES:
THE JEWISH WOMAN IN GRAECO-ROMAN PALESTINE
Léonie J. Archer
61 FROM CHAOS TO RESTORATION:
AN INTEGRATIVE READING OF ISAIAH 24–27
Dan G. Johnson
62 THE OLD TESTAMENT AND FOLKLORE STUDY
Patricia G. Kirkpatrick
63 SHILOH:
A BIBLICAL CITY IN TRADITION AND HISTORY
Donald G. Schley
64 TO SEE AND NOT PERCEIVE:
ISAIAH 6.9-10 IN EARLY JEWISH AND CHRISTIAN INTERPRETATION
Craig A. Evans
65 THERE IS HOPE FOR A TREE: THE TREE AS METAPHOR IN ISAIAH
Kirsten Nielsen
66 SECRETS OF THE TIMES:
MYTH AND HISTORY IN BIBLICAL CHRONOLOGY
Jeremy Hughes
67 ASCRIBE TO THE LORD:
BIBLICAL AND OTHER STUDIES IN MEMORY OF PETER C. CRAIGIE
Edited by Lyle Eslinger & Glen Taylor

68 THE TRIUMPH OF IRONY IN THE BOOK OF JUDGES
Lillian R. Klein
69 ZEPHANIAH, A PROPHETIC DRAMA
Paul R. House
70 NARRATIVE ART IN THE BIBLE
Shimon Bar-Efrat
71 QOHELET AND HIS CONTRADICTIONS
Michael V. Fox
72 CIRCLE OF SOVEREIGNTY:
A STORY OF STORIES IN DANIEL 1–6
Danna Nolan Fewell
73 DAVID'S SOCIAL DRAMA:
A HOLOGRAM OF THE EARLY IRON AGE
James W. Flanagan
74 THE STRUCTURAL ANALYSIS OF BIBLICAL AND CANAANITE POETRY
Edited by Willem van der Meer & Johannes C. de Moor
75 DAVID IN LOVE AND WAR:
THE PURSUIT OF POWER IN 2 SAMUEL 10–12
Randall C. Bailey
76 GOD IS KING:
UNDERSTANDING AN ISRAELITE METAPHOR
Marc Zvi Brettler
77 EDOM AND THE EDOMITES
John R. Bartlett
78 SWALLOWING THE SCROLL:
TEXTUALITY AND THE DYNAMICS OF DISCOURSE
IN EZEKIEL'S PROPHECY
Ellen F. Davies
79 GIBEAH:
THE SEARCH FOR A BIBLICAL CITY
Patrick M. Arnold, S.J.
80 THE NATHAN NARRATIVES
Gwilym H. Jones
81 ANTI-COVENANT:
COUNTER-READING WOMEN'S LIVES IN THE HEBREW BIBLE
Edited by Mieke Bal
82 RHETORIC AND BIBLICAL INTERPRETATION
Dale Patrick & Allen Scult
83 THE EARTH AND THE WATERS IN GENESIS 1 AND 2:
A LINGUISTIC INVESTIGATION
David Toshio Tsumura
84 INTO THE HANDS OF THE LIVING GOD
Lyle Eslinger

85 FROM CARMEL TO HOREB:
ELIJAH IN CRISIS
Alan J. Hauser & Russell Gregory
86 THE SYNTAX OF THE VERB IN CLASSICAL HEBREW PROSE
Alviero Niccacci
Translated by W.G.E. Watson
87 THE BIBLE IN THREE DIMENSIONS:
ESSAYS IN CELEBRATION OF FORTY YEARS OF BIBLICAL STUDIES
IN THE UNIVERSITY OF SHEFFIELD
Edited by David J.A. Clines, Stephen E. Fowl & Stanley E. Porter
88 THE PERSUASIVE APPEAL OF THE CHRONICLER:
A RHETORICAL ANALYSIS
Rodney K. Duke
89 THE PROBLEM OF THE PROCESS OF TRANSMISSION
IN THE PENTATEUCH
Rolf Rendtorff
Translated by John J. Scullion
90 BIBLICAL HEBREW IN TRANSITION:
THE LANGUAGE OF THE BOOK OF EZEKIEL
Mark F. Rooker
91 THE IDEOLOGY OF RITUAL:
SPACE, TIME AND STATUS IN THE PRIESTLY THEOLOGY
Frank H. Gorman, Jr
92 ON HUMOUR AND THE COMIC IN THE HEBREW BIBLE
Edited by Yehuda T. Radday & Athalya Brenner
93 JOSHUA 24 AS POETIC NARRATIVE
William T. Koopmans
94 WHAT DOES EVE DO TO HELP? AND OTHER READERLY QUESTIONS
TO THE OLD TESTAMENT
David J.A. Clines
95 GOD SAVES:
LESSONS FROM THE ELISHA STORIES
Rick Dale Moore
96 ANNOUNCEMENTS OF PLOT IN GENESIS
Laurence A. Turner
97 THE UNITY OF THE TWELVE
Paul R. House
98 ANCIENT CONQUEST ACCOUNTS:
A STUDY IN ANCIENT NEAR EASTERN AND BIBLICAL HISTORY WRITING
K. Lawson Younger, Jr
99 WEALTH AND POVERTY IN THE BOOK OF PROVERBS
R.N. Whybray

116 NARRATIVE AND NOVELLA IN SAMUEL:
STUDIES BY HUGO GRESSMANN AND OTHER SCHOLARS 1906–1923
Translated by David E. Orton
Edited by David M. Gunn

117 SECOND TEMPLE STUDIES:
1. PERSIAN PERIOD
Edited by Philip R. Davies

118 SEEING AND HEARING GOD WITH THE PSALMS:
THE PROPHETIC LITURGY FROM THE SECOND TEMPLE IN JERUSALEM
Raymond Jacques Tournay
Translated by J. Edward Crowley

119 TELLING QUEEN MICHAL'S STORY:
AN EXPERIMENT IN COMPARATIVE INTERPRETATION
Edited by David J.A. Clines & Tamara C. Eskenazi

120 THE REFORMING KINGS:
CULT AND SOCIETY IN FIRST TEMPLE JUDAH
Richard H. Lowery

121 KING SAUL IN THE HISTORIOGRAPHY OF JUDAH
Diana Vikander Edelman

122 IMAGES OF EMPIRE
Edited by Loveday Alexander

123 JUDAHITE BURIAL PRACTICES AND BELIEFS ABOUT THE DEAD
Elizabeth Bloch-Smith

124 LAW AND IDEOLOGY IN MONARCHIC ISRAEL
Edited by Baruch Halpern and Deborah W. Hobson

125 PRIESTHOOD AND CULT IN ANCIENT ISRAEL
Edited by Gary A. Anderson and Saul M. Olyan

126 W.M.L.DE WETTE, FOUNDER OF MODERN BIBLICAL CRITICISM:
AN INTELLECTUAL BIOGRAPHY
John W. Rogerson

127 THE FABRIC OF HISTORY:
TEXT, ARTIFACT AND ISRAEL'S PAST
Edited by Diana Vikander Edelman

128 BIBLICAL SOUND AND SENSE:
POETIC SOUND PATTERNS IN PROVERBS 10–29
Thomas P. McCreesh, OP

129 THE ARAMAIC OF DANIEL IN THE LIGHT OF OLD ARAMAIC
Zdravko Stefanovic

130 STRUCTURE AND THE BOOK OF ZECHARIAH
Michael Butterworth

131 FORMS OF DEFORMITY:
A MOTIF-INDEX OF ABNORMALITIES, DEFORMITIES AND DISABILITIES IN TRADITIONAL JEWISH LITERATURE
Lynn Holden

132 CONTEXTS FOR AMOS:
PROPHETIC POETICS IN LATIN AMERICAN PERSPECTIVE
Mark Daniel Carroll R.

133 THE FORSAKEN FIRSTBORN:
A STUDY OF A RECURRENT MOTIF IN THE PATRIARCHAL NARRATIVES
R. Syrén

135 ISRAEL IN EGYPT:
A READING OF EXODUS 1–2
G.F. Davies

136 A WALK THROUGH THE GARDEN:
BIBLICAL, ICONOGRAPHICAL AND LITERARY IMAGES OF EDEN
Edited by P. Morris and D. Sawyer

137 JUSTICE AND RIGHTEOUSNESS:
BIBLICAL THEMES AND THEIR INFLUENCE
Edited by H. Graf Reventlow & Y. Hoffman

138 TEXT AS PRETEXT:
ESSAYS IN HONOUR OF ROBERT DAVIDSON
Edited by R.P. Carroll

139 PSALM AND STORY:
INSET HYMNS IN HEBREW NARRATIVE
J.W. Watts
Gösta W. Ahlström

147 VOWS IN THE HEBREW BIBLE AND THE ANCIENT NEAR EAST
Tony W. Cartledge

148 IN SEARCH OF ANCIENT ISRAEL
P.R. Davies

151 THE CITIZEN–TEMPLE COMMUNITY
Joel Weinberg